Ten Changes Affecting
Christians Everywhere

Global-
Trends

·····································

Gordon
Aeschliman

INTERVARSITY PRESS
DOWNERS GROVE, ILLINOIS 60515

InterVarsity Press is the book-publishing division of InterVarsity Christian Fellowship, a student movement active on campus at hundreds of universities, colleges and schools of nursing in the United States of America, and a member movement of the International Fellowship of Evangelical Students. For information about local and regional activities, write Public Relations Dept., InterVarsity Christian Fellowship, 6400 Schroeder Rd., P.O. Box 7895, Madison, WI 53707-7895.

All Scripture quotations, unless otherwise indicated, are from the Holy Bible, New International Version. Copyright © 1973, 1978, International Bible Society. Used by permission of Zondervan Bible Publishers.

Cover illustration: Jerry Tiritilli

ISBN 0-8308-1732-8

Printed in the United States of America ∞

Library of Congress Cataloging-in-Publication Data

Aeschliman, Gordon D., 1957-
   GlobalTrends: ten trends affecting Christians everywhere/by Gordon D. Aeschliman.
     p.   cm.
   Includes bibliographical references.
   ISBN 0-8308-1732-8
    1. Christianity—20th century.   2. World politics—1985-1995.
 I. Title. II. Title: Global trends.
 BR481.A47   1990
 270.8'29—dc20   90-47208
                                     CIP

15	14	13	12	11	10	9	8	7	6	5	4	3	2	1
01	00	99	98	97	96	95	94	93	92	91	90			

Introduction

We are living in an unprecedented and explosive day. Never before has the world been so pregnant with the possibility of peace and yet so horribly wracked by poverty, revolution, environmental destruction and despair.

Where to go from here is not an academic question; it's a matter of life and death. Those of us who have eternity alive in our hearts have the awesome privilege of involving ourselves in the pain and promise of the future, bringing with us all the resources of Jesus' kingdom.

The way ahead is uncharted.

Christ has not given us a road map with such simple directions as "turn left here," "stop" or "go for three miles." Our equipment, rather, is a heart fashioned by the love of Jesus; the gifts of the Holy Spirit that enable us to respond in the character of Christ and to serve in our unique ways; a mind that is sharp to perceive and quick to discern; the fellowship of believers who make up for our deficiencies; the Bible, which lights our path and draws us closer to the God we love and serve; the history of the church's attempts to be salt and light; and ears that acutely hear the cries of God's precious creation.

To step inside this world is to accept the call of the most exciting, demanding, delicate and rewarding enterprise available to us. The elite do not qualify. True to God's upside-down approach, the humble and needy riffraff of society will be on the vanguard of this endeavor. That's what this book is all about.

This is not a liberal, let's-find-utopia dream book. That sort of book could only be written by people who only pull their heads out of the sand long enough to punch a manuscript into a computer. Nor is this a right-wing *Megatrends 2000*-type book that ignores the world's suffering. Today's Christians do not have the luxury of identifying themselves under either of these categories. The world is too messy to allow such simple classification.

Instead, our banner is the Lord Jesus Christ, and our allegiance to his ways will continually call us to a higher ground that confounds the wisdom of this world. Christ invites us to join him in his journey of love to all the world. This book is an attempt to sketch out that trajectory on the canvas of our contemporary society.

I was born and reared in the Republic of South Africa. The annual academic diet—in both of the public schools I attended as a child—included a series of lectures on the Great Trek. It was the story of the Dutch settlers' journey northward, beyond the reaches of the British Empire (which had forcibly taken control of the Cape and was working on expansionistic visions to rule all of Africa, from the Cape to Cairo). These lectures recounted the heroic tales of children, women and men who survived encounters with wild beasts, forbidding mountain ranges, debilitating diseases and hostile Black tribes. The great-grandchildren of these pioneers established the Afrikaner, White-run Republic of South Africa. The sacrifices of these trekkers was the main point of the lessons, and their success in establishing the Republic through their offspring was seen as God's blessing for such costly perseverance.

These trekkers' contemporaries included such notables as Sir Richard Burton and David Livingstone. Like the trekkers, these explorers faced seemingly impossible barriers. Yet their courage and persistence led to discoveries that greatly expanded the knowledge and power of the British throne. "God save the Queen!" was the joyous and patriotic response to each progress report.

It has taken more than a century for the ethical implications of these treks to receive the academic attention they deserve. Slavery, racism, economic exploitation, abuse of natural resources and political domination were all common results of these explorations. In addition, memories of glory turned gory as nationals were allowed to recount their versions of the treks. A continent-wide movement for freedom was born, and in only three decades all African countries but South Africa have broken free from European shackles.

The heroic stories of missionaries' entrance to Africa parallel the trekkers' stories. Disease and death were regular companions to these saints who left home and country for the selfless goal of bringing others into the kingdom of God. But just as the governments of the colonial world have been slow to question the ethical basis of their former pursuits, so too often the missionary movement has been slow to accept the input of Black national Christians who have a different perspective on the missionary treks.

Unfortunately, missionaries have too often sided with White views of colonization and have given their blessing to occupying governments that are "bringing civilization to savages." The abuse' of nationals is justified to the point that missionaries have found themselves endorsing South African apartheid, a brutal structure under which hundreds of thousands of Blacks have been oppressed and killed.

Incredible as it seems, Western missionary brochures and prayer letters are still appealing for funds to help spread the gospel in Black South Africa—and to counter the aspirations of "leftist Blacks." One would expect instead an impassioned appeal for funds to help evangelize the Whites, whose oppression of Blacks is a clear indication of their lostness.

As we enter the twenty-first century, evangelical activists who are committed to the global call of God will need to face the ethical questions that go with our past missions endeavors. One response would be simply to write off our missionaries' history as illegitimate, disassociating ourselves from even the positive elements of their service. Another route would be to deny major moral failures—such as those in South Africa—and assume that our view of history does not need correction from national Christians. To embrace either of these extremes would disqualify us from meaningful participation in future missions. Both responses ignore the complex nature of our world. The former position cuts off part of the body of Christ; the latter asserts that Westerners can do no wrong.

Where Do We Go from Here?

Simply put, this is the day of new wineskins. In Luke 5:37-38 Jesus tells his disciples that new wine needs new wineskins. The structure of old Judaism could not contain the good news presented in Jesus Christ. Consequently, the New Testament church was born, and Gentiles from all over the world became heirs with Abraham. Howard Snyder, in *The Problem of Wineskins,* makes the case that God is always a God of newness. "Behold, I make all things new" (Rev 21:5). "Behold, I am doing a new thing; now it springs forth, do you not perceive it?" (Is 43:19). And wherever the gospel goes it *makes* things new; hence, "the gospel itself demands [that we] change."[1]

The world has gone through enormous changes in the past 150 years, yet most of our mission structures reflect very little change. It is possible that our mission to the world is becoming irrelevant. We need the courage to adapt to a new jungle, a new uncharted world in which the accomplishments of the past have produced a global society that desperately needs a new visitation from the people of Jesus. If we're brave enough to let go of the security that old ways of thinking allow, we will have the honor of entering the new territories of the coming century—and of serving the broken and needy inhabitants.

Imagine for a moment that you are with a group of friends at a pizza parlor. One of your friends, Jeremy, suddenly collapses. Together you and your friends rush him to the nearest doctor, who happens to work out of a storefront just a block away. The doctor glances at Jeremy, now unconscious, and says, "No problem; I know just what to do." He immediately cuts into Jeremy's abdomen, removes his kidney, and inserts a new one that had been stored with several others on the shelf. He sews Jeremy up and, to your horror, proclaims the job "done!"

Of course, responsible doctors never would do such a thing. Rather, they would probe for pain or other clues, inquire into family medical history, and seek access to Jeremy's medical records. A careful survey of Jeremy's present condition and history would render the possibility of success much greater.

Facing today's global society is not much different. It is profoundly human, and those who desire to care for it will want to probe for pain, ask personal questions, inquire into family history. We work under the Great Physician, who is expert in his care for society; we will want to follow his lead.

The ten trends discussed in the pages that follow are readings on our world *today,* an attempt to discern the various difficulties and dreams that define the condition of our globe and affect our response as Christians.

1

The Shrinking Globe

With you the dawn has yet to climb to its noontide. History is dense with its events. Every year, every day, every hour is the prolific parent of opportunities that might make angels rejoice, and responsibilities that might make even angels tremble!
ARTHUR TAPPAN PIERSON, 1898[1]

O N one of my recent trips back to Los Angeles from Africa, I had a few hours' layover in Paris. I did what any good tourist would do: I caught a bus downtown for brunch under the shadow of the Arc de Triomphe. At noon I boarded a nonstop flight to L.A.; because of the time change, I was able to get that day's news at home on television. The lead story had to do with a student revolt in Paris. I watched in disbelief as students destroyed the very café in which I had relaxed earlier that day.

Transportation

Modern transportation has brought the world next door. When Jesus told his disciples that they were to be his witnesses in Judea,

Samaria and the uttermost parts of the world, they never dreamed it could be this simple. For them a trek to nearby Galilee took careful planning, the gathering of appropriate food and clothing, and making sure that business would continue as usual in their absence. Today I would travel twice that same distance merely for a forty-five-minute appointment.

In the 1700s a missionary's trip to India or Australia could take up to twelve months, and the possibility of disease and death resulting from the lack of proper nutrition en route was part of the journey. A return trip depended on boat schedules, and a letter home telling of one's safe arrival might arrive three years after the original departure date. Today such a trip can be made in a single day—with meals, beverages and desk provided. A handy airplane telephone lets us confirm that our ride is waiting at the airport.

I can remember going as a ten-year-old from the West Coast of the United States to Johannesburg, South Africa, by the most common and cheapest route: five days by car across the United States; five days by ship to Southampton, England; eleven days by ship to Cape Town; and a final day by train to Johannesburg. That twenty-two-day trip was just a couple of decades ago. This year I can make the same trip in eighteen hours, with one plane change in Europe.

Communications

Communication used to depend on transportation (for the delivery of a letter, for example). In the 1830s the first transatlantic tele-communication cable was successfully laid along the ocean floor. That step in the communications revolution (together with the invention of the telephone) set our globe on a course that will eventually erase all distance.

Computer-operated switchboards send voice memos to three

hundred senior staff members simultaneously. TV networks compete for a two-second lead on breaking international stories. A friend of mine who is house-sitting for an elderly couple from L.A. faxes a message to them in their Scotland vacation spot that the pets are doing fine.

On a whim, I recently telephoned a friend I'd met in Manila. He lives in Nairobi. From my home in Los Angeles, I called directory assistance in Nairobi and was able to get my friend's home phone number.

"How's the weather?" was my first question. (Who needs the television weatherman?)

"Fine," he said. "Hey, I just saw on the TV that you had an earthquake in L.A. today."

I had read in that morning's paper that the Kenyan government had caught several elephant-tusk poachers the day before. "Yes, they've already been sentenced" was my friend's update.

Millions of phone calls across borders and oceans each day trade everything from the latest baseball statistics to cake recipes to information on covert military operations. Distance doesn't affect corporate board meetings: talking heads from around the world are satellite-beamed into the conference room where TV images talk to each other and make critical business decisions. Distance doesn't even affect our entertainment: in 1990, the televised Academy Awards ceremonies broadcast via satellite from six continents.

Fax machines kept the world current on the Chinese government's brutal suppression of student protests in and around Tiananmen Square, and live TV images of U.S. troops invading Panama brought back painful memories of Vietnam, ensuring a quick return of U.S. soldiers. As Eastern Europe's communist governments fell in late 1989, the world received up-to-the-minute coverage. On Sunday, February 11, 1990, I watched Nelson Mandela the very second he stepped into freedom. We were 12,000 miles apart.

Televised images have acquired such power that the "photogenic factor" is an important consideration for would-be presidents and legislators. Ronald Reagan, the "Great Communicator," milked TV and radio technology for all it was worth and set the pace for all who would follow. Scriptwriting and rehearsals are common to job descriptions of corporate presidents as well as preachers.

This new communications technology has introduced a certain impatience. I used to wait happily for some information to arrive by mail; now I stand next to the fax machine and mutter, "C'mon, c'mon," as I watch the same information appear thirty seconds after I requested it. On the other hand, I can't hide behind the "It's in the mail" line anymore. A staff member at our accounting firm says, "Fine, just fax me what you mailed." He, too, wants it *now*.

Economic Tango

International transportation and communication technologies suddenly make cheap labor more accessible. As one consequence, a number of workers have lost their jobs to citizens of another country across the globe. Some economists speak of the formation of an international labor pool, in which people around the world are competing for the same low-paying jobs.[2]

For example, try to buy a car made entirely in the U.S.A.—it's impossible. The international auto has arrived. James Risen, staff writer for the *Los Angeles Times,* describes the situation well:

> Peugeot . . . has formed a joint venture with an industrial company in India to produce French-designed pickup trucks near Bombay.

Peugeot's announcement came the same week that Chrysler unveiled a double-barreled plan not only to link up with Renault of France, but Hyundai of South Korea as well. . . . Toyota of Japan announced that it is seriously considering building passenger cars in Britain.

The globalization of the auto industry . . . has arrived. . . .

Between them, General Motors, Ford and Chrysler are selling cars in North America that are assembled in Japan, South Korea, Mexico, Thailand, Taiwan, West Germany and Italy, as well as cars built by joint ventures with Japanese auto makers in the United States and Canada.[3]

The stock market is marked by the same interrelationships. When one exchange ripples, the rest feel the waves. So tight are these relationships that after the October 19, 1987, stock market crash in the United States, Tokyo and Hong Kong temporarily shut down their exchanges to avoid a similar fall.

In *Current History* magazine, Jeffrey Gasten describes how U.S. foreign policy is affected by international trade agreements and so-called economic super blocs—multinational trading blocs that have centered in North America, Western Europe and East Asia.[4] Western Europe has been making plans to become the world's fourth largest economic center in 1992. And although developments in Eastern Europe are expected to have some impact on those plans, trade agreements across international borders are seen as the key to their success.

Trade between the United States and Asia has grown rapidly; at present, the harbors of Los Angeles and Long Beach combined receive double the amount of freight going into New York. The West Coast of the United States will take on much more of an international flavor as a consequence.

Even newly emerged democracies are getting into the economic dance. The new leaders of Eastern European countries are telling Western governments that they should not celebrate the formation of Western-style democracies unless they are willing to support those democracies with dollars. Conservative politicians in the United States, concerned that their rhetoric about the advantages of a democracy in Nicaragua will be proved false by an economic failure, are requesting millions of aid dollars for that country. The point is made: Democracy in Nicaragua cannot survive without international economic involvement. And Nicaragua is not alone. Close to one billion dollars will be diverted from other Third World projects into Panama to prop up the U.S.-installed government, which cannot survive on democratic ideology alone.

We Are the World

The world is shrinking: several hundred thousand internationals move into Los Angeles County each year, creating minivillages that make the place a virtual United Nations showcase; a day's trip across Europe puts one in contact with dozens of ethnic groups, including Turks, Malaysians, Algerians and Chinese; Middle Eastern oil industries hire and transport thousands of Asian laborers; the Amazon's interior road system is largely the product of Chinese enterprise. What used to be unfamiliar, distant faces seen by North Americans only in *National Geographic* and on public-television specials are now the faces of our grocer, tax consultant, mechanic and next-door neighbor.

These factors have produced a sort of world culture. The town square is no longer reserved for the Fourth of July parade. Rather, it is the place where peoples of all nations are getting together. All the world now lives next door.

I was in Asia for three weeks just after the record "We Are the World" was released. Within days, bootlegged versions with Asian voice tracks were blasting from vendor stands in Bombay, Bangkok, and Hong Kong. Live Aid, the British organization that pulled together artists around the goal of raising funds to combat Ethiopian famine, played to more than a billion listeners simultaneously, uniting global youth in the new town-square parade. We *are* the world; if one doubts the truth of those words, one need only look around.

The current freedom movements around the world have been helped by the shrinking globe. Chinese students revolting in Tiananmen Square displayed English-language banners for the sake of the Western press.[5] The major U.S. television news anchors traveled from China to Soweto to the Berlin Wall because of the importance of the events in each of these places; their viewers demanded an accurate, personal picture.

A new world music has emerged that combines the Bob Dylan sound of the 1960s and boldly prophetic lyrics with a mix of Latin, African and Middle Eastern melodies and rhythms. Amy Duncan observes that in the 1990s, "one can't help but be struck by the fact that 'music as an international language' has become less a cliché and more a reality."[6]

The *Detroit Free Press* tells its Michigan readers that preparing for the nineties will require learning Spanish and the metric system,[7] while in a village a thousand miles up the Amazon, people are reading the French-owned fashion magazine *Elle* and the U.S.-produced *Better Homes & Gardens.* Guatemalans are ordering chicken chow mein, American youth are wearing Russian designer jeans, the Japanese are displaying their latest cuts at top Paris fashion shows and the French are eating Big Macs.

This Is Our World

Perhaps the most important adjustment we need to make, given this shrinking globe, is in our perception of "home." We are all family. "They" are not intruders; rather, they are "us." Our natural tendency is to build walls around ourselves and protect our world from outsiders. What we are actually trying to protect is the way things *were*—like insisting on riding a horse to work even though the car has been around for ninety years. Our world has changed. That's simply a fact. Learning to adapt to that fact is simply a good idea.

But we don't have to view adaptation as an obligation. Appreciating the beauty of a flower bed dotted with dozens of colors and plants is not a duty; it's a pleasure. So it is with our new multicolored, multicultured home. We have the pleasure of seeing God's human creation in its diverse extremes, complementing one another, displaying the splendor of a masterpiece that used every conceivable mix of the Artist's paints. This is God's gift to us.

This phenomenon is to the church's benefit. Never before have the words of the apostle John been so poignant: "Let us not love with words or tongue but with actions and in truth" (1 Jn 3:18). If the gospel has truly come alive in us, then our living will become the irresistible aroma of Christ that draws men and women to the deep well of true love. Rather than feeling threatened, we can take the opportunity to shed our fears of the international community and draw closer to the truth.

I spent ten years of my life living three miles outside Soweto. Apartheid ensured that the average White citizen would never pass through that city of a million-plus residents. Not one of my White South African friends had ever been inside Soweto; they believed their parents' and grandparents' warnings that Soweto was a cesspool of Black liberals, communist-inspired revolutionaries, rapists, bums. Had any of these Whites ventured to lift the color curtain, they would have discovered a healthy, thriving Black church that puts most White worship to shame. Soweto was God's gift to Johannesburg, but fear of God's creation kept that gift wrapped up for more than a century.

A Question of Opportunity

As we contemplate our shrinking globe, we must recognize the growing opportunity for the gospel's advance. A. T. Pierson, chief recorder of the Western missionary movement in the nineteenth century, saw his world so packed with opportunity that he referred to it as a *crisis:* a "combination of grand opportunity and great responsibility; chance of glorious success or awful failure."[8] Indeed, Pierson's century *was* a grand time. The 1800s broke open the world with exploration and colonization, making it accessible as never before. The 1830s produced technological breakthroughs, including the first transatlantic steamboat and transatlantic tele-communications. Government treaties were made with Japan and China in 1854 and 1856, respectively, opening the way for increased missionary activity (not least of which was Hudson Taylor's new mission in 1865). Livingstone and Stanley "opened" Africa to the West, and the secular press threw in its support and published their findings.

To many mission leaders, these strides forward signaled the final era of world history and, hence, the greatest moment of missionary endeavor. Yet as the 1800s gave way to the 1900s, the Student Volunteer Movement suddenly burst forth, and perhaps as many as 30,000 young adults left U.S. shores for distant lands. The West has not seen anything like it since.

Pierson's generation could not have known the opportunities God would offer the following generations. Never before has the shadow of the church been cast so far into distant places. Every tribe created by the hand of God now lives within the reach of

Christians, be it through commerce, education, medicine or government.

Our hour is unprecedented, our jungle is uncharted, our opportunities are unmatched. There is only one village left in our day, and it is called *Planet Earth*. To be a member of God's international family as humanity steps into the twenty-first century is perhaps the closest we will get to heaven in the flesh.

chapter 2

The Islamic Revolution

IF the shrinking globe brings Christianity its greatest opportunity for service, fundamentalist Islam brings it the single greatest challenge in the coming decade. Islam will be to the nineties as Marxism was to the post-World War 2 era.

When Marxism seemed a genuine threat, it was tempting to make it the source of political evil in the world. We are often guided by our hates and fears rather than by what we love and respect. But now the great specter of communism is vanishing. Many believe the leading candidate to take communism's place is Islam. However, Christians should not be quick to apply to Muslims the hates and fears that surrounded our understanding of communists. Our concern should be to ask how we can sensitively enter into the issues of Muslims' lives and unveil Jesus Christ to them.

Misconceptions

In much of the world, Islam conjures images of exploding airplanes, barracks being blown up by suicide crusaders, cruise-ship passengers being shot and dumped overboard, and holy men calling their nations to rise and destroy the "Great Satan" of America. These images clearly set the stage for our protectionist attitudes and crazed-Islam stereotypes.

We in the free world never really understood why so many nations turned to Marxism. We missed the cries of the common people who found in Marxism symbols of hope and liberation. So it is with Islam. We need to put aside our offense at frequently being labeled a "Great Satan" (because we oppose the "good" these people are seeking). We need to understand the people of this global religion that is currently second only to Christianity in its number of followers.

From an outsider's viewpoint, Islam's conquests after the Prophet Muhammad's death in A.D. 632 were not too different from Israel's vanquishing of the inhabitants of the Promised Land. Contemporaries of Joshua would have described the Hebrew conquest as one that consumed women, beasts and children. Following the death of Muhammad, Arab armies raced through Europe, Northern Africa, the Middle East, and Southwestern Asia, and within one hundred years were found in China. The movement has grown to encompass much greater parts of Africa and Asia and stretches of Oceania. In fact, Islam's only places of territorial retreat since have been Spain and Italy.

The Qur'an, Islam's holy book, is not a manual for war. It calls for Muslims to fight, but to fight defensively: "Fight for the sake of

Allah those who fight against you, but do not attack them first. Allah does not love the aggressors" (II:190). And Islam does not carry an inherent racism; the Qur'an's teaching is that all were created from a "single soul" (IV:1).

Scientific and cultural contributions to our world, arising from the followers of Islam, include the invention of the 365-day calendar, algebra, the discovery of alkali, the diagnosis of measles and smallpox, documentation of the basics of pulmonary circulation, grape grafting, and a unique form of architecture that in California today is referred to as "contemporary Spanish."[1]

Islam's Reach

Thirty-eight countries are more than fifty per cent Muslim. One person in every five in the world is Muslim. India has 100 million Muslims; fourteen per cent of all immigrants to the United States are Muslim; the Soviet Union's total population is almost 20 per cent Muslim; and Albania, the most closed society in the world, is 62.5 per cent Muslim.

The march of Islam has—until recently—gone largely unnoticed. Until the early 1970s, it was a slow brush fire that steadily went its course. And although Muammar Qaddafi and the Ayatollah Khomeini and others of their ilk, have drawn much attention to Islam in our day, their contributions alone do not explain the sudden success of Islam. Responsibility for the recent boost falls to the simple word *oil.* The influx of petrodollars in the seventies gave Islam a worldwide presence, in a fashion best understood as a cross between the economic rise of Great Britain in the 1800s and the evangelistic fervor of Marxists in the 1900s.

A mere fifteen years ago, Arab leaders discovered that oil made them billionaires. Garages were built for fleets of Rolls Royces, hangars were erected for private jets, and palaces were constructed for vacations. Entire cities were created from scratch (much to the delight of Western engineering companies), and Arab youth set off to explore Western civilization. In short, it was party time.

But something significant was happening at these parties. There were many discussions of Allah's obvious blessings. That perspective combined with the Arabs' history of suffering: their humiliation at the hands of Israel since 1948; the one-sided position of Western powers against the Arabs in this struggle; and their reputation as head-in-the-sand tent dwellers. These injuries set the stage for an all-out religious crusade that would tell the world how blessed they were in Allah's eyes and return to them their dignity and status.

Millions of dollars were poured into evangelism, the creation of mosques and schools, and the construction of missionary centers—including $40-million centers in New York and Ohio. Specific strategies have included the election of Muslims to public office and the observance of Islamic holy days in public schools. London has more than 1,000 Muslim worship centers, and several suburbs have school boards run entirely by Muslims.

In Black America and Africa, Islam's promise of racial equality where Western racism has persisted brings hundreds of thousands into the fold. A more subtle yet even stronger pull has been the imaging of the West as evil and elevation of the African way as superior. Appeals to national pride, self-reliance and self-worth are key evangelistic tools for these Islamic missionary bands, which are enjoying tremendous success in their efforts.

Enter the Revolutionaries

The Scriptures teach us that God causes kings to rise and fall. We must wonder what would have become of modern-day Islam had certain "kings" not arisen.

The Ayatollah Khomeini's June 1989 funeral marked the fall of one such king, whose ten-year reign set Islam on its current course. Two million mourners came to his funeral. In a frenzied farewell to their leader, 8 were crushed to death, 440 were hospitalized, and another 10,800 suffered injuries.[2]

It was Khomeini's charismatic skills, his perception of people, his grasp of the sociopolitical implications of Islam, and his raw leadership gifts combined with gutsy ambition that catapulted him to his religious throne. While in exile, he captured the imaginations of his people and, in their minds, managed to link the Shah of Iran's government with all the evils of the West. Oil dollars had brought in not only Western technology and modernization but also the CIA-trained Savak, a terror-inducing secret-police band of 4,000 men who tortured those opposing the Shah's leadership.

The Shah was eventually forced to flee, and Khomeini stepped into the national void, where he began building his world platform. "Islam is political or it is nothing," said Khomeini, and he brought all of Iran under the rulership of Allah. *Islam* means "submission," and Khomeini preached total submission. He interpreted Mohammed's vision of life to mean that *religious leaders* are to control all aspects of living because they are God's servants. Hence, "Islam is not only a faith. It is a complete way of life, an articulate platform for political action, and a vigorous program for ordering society. The prophet Mohammed founded not only a community, but also a polity, a sovereign state and an empire."[3]

Khomeini led the way for the radical elements and passions of Islam to flourish. He denounced technological progress (the key to modernism) and political liberalism (the source of democracy; as might be expected, only two of today's forty-five Muslim countries are democracies).[4] So forceful was Khomeini's leadership that he could send one million children to their deaths as they defended the border against Iraq (in the name of Allah); Americans were held hostage for 444 days under his watch; the remains of servicemen from a failed Delta-Force rescue attempt were gleefully displayed on national television; the assassination of British author Salman Rushdie was ordered by his decree; and terrorist activities, in the name of a holy war against infidels, were financed from his coffers.

Other leaders have emerged on the Islamic world scene, including Qaddafi, Assad and Hussein, but none has had the influence of Khomeini. Qaddafi has certainly worked at developing his influence, but his power has emerged more from money than from his rallying skills. His inability to perceive public sentiment is probably best illustrated by his diplomatic exchanges with Romania's Nicolae Ceausescu only two weeks before the latter's inglorious trial and execution.

Islam's leaders are not selfless servants. Empire building and international competition have prolonged feuds that continue to kill hundreds. Warring factions claim that they are the true embodiment of Islam and that death is a small sacrifice to ask of those in pursuit of the true faith. And Islam's battle with the unconverted far outweighs, in Muslim minds, any internal fighting.

But where will such evangelistic battles lead, and what fronts will be won? Where will the new missions be founded? Who will rise up to be the new prophets of Islam? And more important, what constitutes an appropriate Christian response to the challenge of this powerful religion?

Where Goes the Revolution?

For now, the main energy for Islamic efforts will come from groups in Iran, Iraq, Libya and Syria. (Saudi Arabia, a country friendly to Western governments, provides a positive, stabilizing force in the

Middle East.) Iran's and Libya's roles will be more forceful and more celebrity-centered in the memory of the late Khomeini and the person of Qaddafi. And Hussein's invasion of Kuwait bolsters significantly his role in the expansionistic designs of the Islamic Revolution. Together these countries are the nerve center of organized efforts to advance Islam, in "assisting Muslim minorities, in pressuring governments to modify their domestic and foreign policies, in helping autonomist Muslim movements, and in inspiring Islamic sentiments far beyond their national boundaries."[5] We are looking at a massive, well-funded Islamic Pentagon that is accountable to no one.

Success has already been achieved in Africa, the Islamic continent of the world. More than forty per cent of its inhabitants are Muslim, and at the current growth rates, the twenty-first century will greet a continent that is more than half Muslim.

Slightly more than 100 million Muslims live in India (twelve per cent of the population). However, the history of Muslim conflict with the Hindus is violent and continuous. Mahatma Gandhi, the world's most famous peace activist, was murdered by fellow Hindus because they saw his peace mission as providing an open door to Muslims and threatening Hindu sovereignty over India. Godse, the seventy-year-old coordinator of the assassination plot, said, "We had no personal reason to do what was done to Gandhi. It was national integrity which forced us to do it."[6] Islamic ideals aside, the fact that more than 60 per cent of India's Muslims live below the poverty line makes for conditions and rhetoric that are friendly to revolutionary agendas.

It is the Soviet Union that will face the most difficult challenges of the Islamic revolution. Accounts of its history of oppression are being passed down from one Muslim generation to the next. All five Central Asian Soviet republics were at one point independent

Muslim states. During the past century, they were taken over by Russian armies. Stalin's forced collectivization increased the bitterness of the populace; memories of the outrages he perpetrated continue to fuel Soviet Muslims' desire for retribution.[7] The Soviet invasion of neighboring Afghanistan (a country that is ninety-nine per cent Muslim) in 1979 sealed the Russians' image as the Asian version of the "Great Satan." The revolution is rumbling.

With this oppressive history and the fact that the USSR is almost twenty per cent Muslim, Soviet leadership is about to experience a volcano that will make the stress produced by *perestroika* and *glasnost* in Latvia, Estonia and Lithuania seem a mere summer storm. Already Muslims have created their own holy places because government restrictions prevent them from making the pilgrimage to Mecca. Tombs of Muslim leaders killed by Russians have become Mecca, sites for political discussions in which the sentiment is predictably anti-Soviet.[8] In 1989 just eight per cent of Soviets identified themselves as card-carrying communists; in the context of the current Islamic revolution, it is not difficult to see the significance of the twenty per cent of Soviets who are Muslims.

Just south of the five Soviet Muslim republics is the doorway to Asia's Islamic revolution. The 52 million Soviet Muslims are company to an additional 380 million Muslims in Southern Asia alone. Of those nine southern nations, five—Afghanistan, Pakistan, Bangladesh, Maldives and Iran—have Islamic governments.

In the Western free world, Islam's presence will be experienced much as the arrival of ethnic minorities was. (There are currently 5 million Muslims in the United States and Canada combined, and there are 13 million [three per cent] in Europe.) Occasional public stirs will arise when Islamic groups fight for their rights to veiled dress, diets free of pork, and observance of Islamic holy days in the workplace. In France, a nation known for its tolerance, these types of demands kicked in a widespread debate that went all the way to the National Assembly. A radio talk show in Paris asked the question "Should we fear the Islamic veil?" Seventy-seven per cent of respondents gave an emotional "Yes."[9]

Journalist Richard Ostling predicts that by 2020 Muslims will be the second largest religious group in the United States, Christians being the first.[10] In the States, the wild card is Louis Farrakhan's Nation of Islam. Urban despair, drug abuse and economic hardship have become symbols for Farrakhan's denunciation of White systemic racism that can be overcome only through Black brotherhood and hatred of Whites. John Perkins, a Black evangelical activist, fears that holy killing, a sort of urban jihad, is very likely the next step in Farrakhan's program; that is, Blacks would kill Whites to avenge society's racism.[11] Not every country will readily accept Islam. Central and South America have provided little foothold to Islam in the past. Less than one-fifth of one per cent of the residents of these regions are Muslim adherents. Of course, no one can predict what will come, but experimentation with democracy, the burgeoning call for justice from the Roman Catholic Church, and the rapidly growing Pentecostal movement appear to leave little room for Islamic inroads.

The Way Ahead

As stated in the opening of this chapter, Islam will present the twenty-first century's greatest challenge to the Christian church. Islam cannot be ignored; it will not simply go away. Yet, head-to-head confrontation is not the solution. In the years ahead, we Christians will need to seriously equip ourselves to positively respond to the challenge that Islam raises.

Step one for Christians is simply to love Muslims and their wonderful cultures. They have a rich heritage of art, science, poetry, music, cooking and commerce. To be sure, every culture has its evil, and Islam is not excepted. This shouldn't blind us, however, to the beauty of these cultures.

Step two is to delve into the history of Islam. Become a student of its revolutions and expansions and retreats. Learn of the noble and ignoble moments. Trace its pathways to the current decade— paths marked by charismatic personalities, powers, and simple people.

Step three is to learn its holy ways. Study the Qur'an, the prayers, the pilgrimage to Mecca, the alms for the poor, the Prophet and the call to war. Include Muslims in your circle of teachers. Respect them, and they will respect your desire to learn.

Step four is to look for understanding of their current ways of life. What are their woes, hardships, joys, aspirations and socio-economic realities? What inspires them and moves them to action? What do they resist?

If God seems to be calling you to live among Muslims, link up with other Christians and organizations that can get you where Muslims are living. No Lone Rangers are encouraged to go down this road. God has always worked through his *people*—families, tribes, congregations, teams. Each of us desperately needs the gifts, wisdom and fellowship of others.

However, all of us can reach out to Muslims, whether or not we move into their neighborhoods or nations. Western society has not established a good track record of just dealings with Muslims. Their image of the "Great Satan" will be a barrier whenever Whites enter their world. We can start to change this by challenging our governments to give just treatment to those Muslims who live in our society.

One of the best examples I have encountered in this area was the action of Robert Douglas, director of the Zwemer Institute for Muslim Studies, an evangelical organization created to serve Christians who want to reach Muslims. The U.S. government arrested six Palestinians in Los Angeles without stating the charges. These five men and one woman were detained for several days before their trial. When the judge was to hear the federal government's case, Douglas drove down to the court building and joined the mostly Muslim crowd of protesters outside, shouting slogans decrying foul play and calling for justice. The *Los Angeles Times* published a letter Douglas wrote to the editor of the paper, which outlined the government's unjust treatment and called for fairness. Robert Douglas's actions did not go unnoticed.

People do not generally risk their lives in dangerous revolutions unless living conditions beg for an escape or noble visions of peoplehood beckon. In the United States, the Nation of Islam will persist as long as racist decisions are handed down by judges, prisons are disproportionately filled with ethnics, inner-city schools get low-grade service, and ghettos are policed by bigoted law-enforcement officers. I don't believe that government has all the answers. But, clearly, injustices that are structurally reinforced require persistent efforts on the part of concerned people to ensure that all the nation's citizens have equal access to the opportunities of the land.

In this regard, Christians need to pray for the governments of the Soviet Union and India. Injustices are a part of their histories, and visions of peoplehood and pure religion cloud the issues to the degree that peace talks are rendered almost impossible. God has raised national Christian leaders in these countries who are pleading the cause of the oppressed before government. It's in the interests of those awaiting the kingdom of God that government institute just laws—a single stroke of the pen can release much of the pressure and relieve the tension that makes bloody revolution inevitable.

I believe that God loves Muslims with a special tenderness and longs to draw them into his family. I pray that he will free us from our racism. I pray that he will plant his seed of love in our hearts and that we will find ourselves strangely warmed by the thought of entering into Muslim lives. And I pray that scores of Christians will end up living in distant and wonderful cultures where our sensitive service will build a stairway from their hearts to heaven.

3

Reaching the World's Poor

I still remember my first encounter with abject poverty. I was in Ethiopia. The year was 1985. The ghastly human suffering I saw there shook my consciousness and burned its images into my mind's eye. I cannot—will not—forget.

I was at a camp of more than 90,000 refugees. One afternoon an additional 26,000 refugees arrived. They had walked for three days and were winding their way down a mountain to a narrow dirt path that led into the camp. I did not want to allow myself the luxury of ignoring this human pain. I stood in the middle of the narrow path for hours as thousands of refugees milled past me, bumping my shoulders, brushing against my body. Husbands carried dead wives, mothers carried dead children. Festering sores, bloated stomachs, moans, groans, dirt, nakedness, hollow eyes. The ugly reality of poverty brushed against me that day and permanently changed my world view.

Early the next morning, I left my tent to survey the vast plain where more than 100,000 refugees had spent the night. Rain had come, and families huddled together in little pyramids with their clothes draped over their heads. Exhaustion and malnutrition had ill prepared these refugees for facing the night's elements, and babies shook with fever all around me.

Mine was the only White face on the plain; a mother figured I could help her. She thrust her sick baby up to my face and begged in a language I couldn't understand. Her piercing scream drew other refugees with victims of the night in their arms, and soon I was surrounded by hundreds of pleading, crawling, grabbing human beings. In confusion, desperation and pain I pushed my way through the pitiful crowd, making my way to my tent, where I attempted to hide. I could shut out the view but not the noise. It was weeks before I could reconcile my feelings of guilt surrounding their starvation and eat normal amounts of food once again.

People need not visit Ethiopia to confront the ravages of poverty. One of every five human beings on the earth lives in poverty. When these 1.2 billion people (five times the size of the U.S. population) go to sleep at night, their bed is the dirt floor—they might not have a roof overhead, they might not have eaten that day. Should they fall ill during the night, no doctor will serve them. When the sun rises they will repeat their daily search for firewood, potable water and employment. Forty million of them are children who will die during their next twelve months of hunger and disease.

Poverty is no simple problem with a single solution. It results from a complex and tragic combination of factors such as war, disease, crop failure, crime, lack of education and medical care, and national debt—to name a few. Christians naturally will want to find their role in this desperate situation.

Save the Children

The young cannot wait for global problems to be solved before they receive the attention and care necessary for their survival. Their needs are immediate; their numbers are widespread.[1]

Children from birth to five years of age are in a crucial developmental stage, and any complications during this critical time only worsen the later effects of poverty. Brain damage, crippled limbs and disease exacerbate the already overwhelming problems. UNICEF's 1990 *State of the World's Children* report says,

A nation in which . . . a third of all children are failing to grow up in mind and body is a nation whose economic and social progress is being sapped from within. Yet many developing nations are exactly in that position. And that is why it is now widely acknowledged that improvements in national health are a cause as well as a consequence of overall development.[2]

One of the most common causes of death in children is diarrhea. Each year, a simple technique called oral rehydration treatment (ORT) is now saving more than one million children who would otherwise have died because of diarrhea and dehydration; it is widely thought that the technique, applied on a broader scale, could save another 2.5 million children annually. The United Nations is vigorously promoting this approach; so far, thirty-six per cent of developing countries are using ORT (up from eleven per cent in 1984).

Today, more than 150 million children less than five years old suffer from malnutrition. Attention focused on their specific needs will greatly diminish the world's poverty level by the end of this decade.

Save the Women

An estimated one-half million women die every year in childbirth, and an additional five hundred per day die due to complications from illegal abortions.[3]

The chances of a woman's dying in childbirth are fifty per cent greater if she becomes pregnant before she is eighteen. However, fifty per cent and forty per cent of eighteen-year-olds in Africa and Asia, respectively, are already married. This situation indicates that culturally sensitive birth-control methods are a critical need if this form of poverty is to be addressed.

It is a fact that impoverished mothers who bear children less than two years apart must endure more physically. The mental and physical burden of providing for babies while trying to survive is harmful to everyone concerned. Again, birth-control methods could prevent this increased suffering and, in addition, would greatly improve the lives of children who *are* born, because the parents would be able to invest much more quality time and care in a smaller number of children.

Current trends indicate that the world's population will reach 7 billion by the year 2025. If women could make the choice of birth control, however, it is estimated that by that year global population would reach only 5.7 billion.[4]

Education and Literacy

The World Conference on Education for All that assembled March 5-9, 1990, in Thailand issued a declaration on education. Its preamble highlights the following poverty-related statistics:

☐ More than 150 million children have no access to primary schooling.

☐ More than 960 million adults, two-thirds of whom are women, are illiterate.

☐ More than one-third of the world's adults have no access to the printed knowledge, new skills and technologies that could improve their lives and help them shape and adapt to social and cultural change.[5]

The previous year, an International Task Force on Literacy met in India in October to suggest principles for both government and nongovernmental organizations for the eradication of poverty through literacy training. The overview section of the document begins:

Mass illiteracy is inextricably linked with mass poverty, structural injustice and marginalization. Therefore, people need to be empowered as learners to get access to the education and knowledge which will enable them both to assume control over their processes of growth, and to become active, responsible participants in a systematic process of social development.[6]

The document explains that much poverty is the consequence of exploitation by those in power. Provision of not only the technical skills of reading and writing but also the social and analytical skills (especially for women and children) will make oppression less likely.

The number of illiterate people is increasing. From 1960 to 1980, the number of illiterate men grew by 20 million, and the number of illiterate women by 74 million. Africa is 70 per cent illiterate; Asia is 40 per cent.[7] As might be expected, the twenty most literate nations are Western, and the twenty least literate nations are African (fourteen) and Asian (six).

Living Water

Unsafe water causes the deaths of perhaps 25 million people per year. Sixty per cent of those deaths involve children under five.

"Water," says Howard Malmstadt in the book *Target Earth*, "is essential for life. It accounts for 50-75% of our body weight, 90% of our blood plasma, 75% of muscle tissue and even 25% of 'dry' bone tissue."[8]

The first problem is to find any water at all; the second is to find *good* water. Almost 80 per cent of all Third World diseases are caused by bad water. The impact on poverty includes lower work productivity, high medical bills, poor quality of living and financial instability. Frank Kaleb Jansen, editor of *Target Earth,* states, "When Jesus asked us to give water to the thirsty, He meant pure, healthy water, not a contaminated, disease-bringing poisonous liquid. Therefore, it is a Christian calling and duty to heal bad water as the prophet Elisha did (2 Kings 2:19-22)."[9]

Fifty-nine nations report that they have access to safe water for under fifty per cent of their citizens. Of the twenty nations with the least access to clean water, sixteen are African, three Asian and one Western (Haiti). Of the twenty nations with the most access to clean water (ninety-five per cent and better), seventeen are Western, one Asian and two African.

Other Poverty Indicators

Gross national product, food production, availability of newspapers, and access to health services, housing, and employment are all additional factors by which poverty can be measured. And, of course, all these factors are linked with one another.

"Well, who's suffering the most?" one might ask. As we've seen so far, the nations experiencing the most poverty are consistently African and Asian. World study groups have gone several steps further by assembling "suffering indexes" that take into account an even larger number of variables than can be addressed here.

One index, titled the "International Human Suffering Index" and produced by the Population Crisis Committee, finds twenty Western nations to have the *lowest* suffering index and sixteen African and four Asian countries to have the *highest* suffering index. The "Quality of Life Index," which takes into account three measures of "quality of life," names twenty Western nations as having the *highest* quality of life and eighteen African and two Asian countries as having the *lowest* quality.

Bryant Myers, director of World Vision's international research division, combines the "International Human Suffering Index" with statistics on adherents to non-Christian religions—coming up with yet another way to measure poverty. Myers and his team have included such categories as material poverty, spiritual poverty, isolation, physical weakness, vulnerability and powerlessness. Africa and Asia still dominate this list, and a little of Latin America slips in.

All of these charts and statistics are simply indicators of the desperate poverty that hounds twenty per cent of our human family each day. They are different brush strokes on the canvas of pain, providing a little more definition and direction to our service of love.

Theories abound on why people suffer so. Unfortunately, many of these theories are born from political preferences rather than genuine concern. Just as the challenge of Islam will require us to enter new jungles and let go of old categories, so the plight of the least among us will call for a fresh approach that incorporates the best thinking across the conservative-liberal continuum. An excellent document that attempts just that was produced in January of 1990: "The Oxford Declaration on Christian Faith and Economics" (see Appendix).

For those who are called to vocations of service to the world's poor, first-rate international community-development programs are available from secular institutions such as the University of

California at Los Angeles and Christian schools such as Eastern College.

The number of the world's poor will continue to increase as population growth continues to add hundreds of thousands of malnourished, undereducated, sick little children to our world's slums and urban centers. It is true that the rich are getting richer and the poor are getting poorer. The existence of one billion poor in our backyard places an ethical demand on the Western church that will be a great challenge to meet, given the luxury our culture offers those who can turn their backs on "the least of these."

chapter 4

The Earth Groans

CARE for the earth, says sociologist Tony Campolo, is the ultimate pro-life issue. If the earth goes, we all go.

To sum up: Islam requires the Christian church to engage in difficult spiritual battles; poverty demands of the church the most costly lifestyle choices; and the earth begs the church to embrace the mandate for stewardship of God's good creation.

The jump from praying only for the salvation of souls to working, as well, for the survival of the soil is perhaps the most challenging theological task evangelicals face in the coming decade. And yet these two extremes are really the arms that wrap themselves around the substance that makes up our call to global mission.

On one level, caring for the earth is actually a simple biblical concept—it's a reflection of love for God.

My three small children enjoy building gadgets and buildings and vehicles out of cardboard, blocks, chairs, blankets and whatever else they can get their hands on. It's a sure bet that my next venture into our living room will put me smack in the middle of their creations. If I walk into the room, ignore their careful efforts, and smash their gadgets into the carpet, I will have made a clear statement about my lack of love for them.

So too with God. The earth is the masterpiece of the Artist, who experimented and labored with shapes, colors, combinations, landscapes and living things. Finally he was satisfied: "It's *great!*" And on the seventh day he rested.

Because we love God, we also love his creation. We treat it with tenderness and dignity. We admire it.

When God created the world, he crafted a place of both beauty and sustenance. Man and Woman could walk through their garden during the cool of the evening and listen to the birds compete in chorus, hear the waterfall rush to its destination and watch the flowers close themselves to the night air in preparation for sleep. And Man and Woman could select fruits and vegetables for their own enjoyment, eating their fill.

God created this relationship of mutual dependency—the one tilled and the other provided. But in their arrogance and independence of spirit, Man and Woman not only took dominion over the earth, they trampled it. The outcome has been harmful to all.

A Lesson from Easter Island

We are seeing the consequences of humanity's harm more clearly in this final decade of the twentieth century, not because our generation is the first to disregard God's handiwork, but rather because our sheer numbers and technological machinery give us greater power to do so destructively.

A poignant environmental lesson comes from pre-industrial times, from the Polynesian society that settled Easter Island in A.D. 400. Situated 2,300 miles west of Chile, this idyllic Pacific island haven had deteriorated by the year 1500 to a colony of vicious, starving cannibals existing on a decimated landscape.[1] What happened?

The islanders, upon arrival, began to clear the land of its logs to build canoes and to use as rollers to erect thirty-seven-foot statues made of lava (weighing up to eighty-five tons each). Such drastic deforestation—for the sake of more than 1,000 statues—led to soil erosion, lower crop yields, a depletion of logs for fishing canoes, and finally starvation. Cannibalism became the means for survival. Over time, factions developed, rival statues were torn down, the defeated were eaten, and in the end only one-third of the population remained.

Today, the United States has five per cent of the world's population. Yet Americans consume twenty-six per cent of the world's oil, release twenty-six per cent of the world's nitrogen oxides, and produce twenty-two per cent of the world's carbon-dioxide emissions.[2] "Tragic failures become moral sins only if one should have known better from the outset," remarks environmentalist Jared Diamond. "The past was still a golden age, but of ignorance, while the present is an Iron Age of willful blindness."[3] The question must be asked: Are we in the States leading a world parade toward a modern-day Easter Island?

Environmental concerns today most often have to do with pollution, deforestation and the loss of species. Recent interest in the environment has given rise to several excellent guides, workbooks and technical manuals on these issues. Because we cannot, in one chapter, begin to approach environmental issues in depth, I have highlighted what I believe to be the most relevant topics. Readers should treat these highlighted topics as a springboard for further study.

Back to Poverty

The poor are most vulnerable to the abuse of the environment. Ron Sider of Evangelicals for Social Action states the relationship succinctly:

> The poor suffer the most. They suffer from reduced food production, toxic wastes that the rich do not want in their neighborhoods, unproductive land, and polluted rivers. . . . Unless we can redirect economic growth in a way that dramatically reduces environmental decay, it will be impossible to expand economic growth in poor nations.[4]

The poor tend to live in villages and have a direct dependency on the land. Poisons and other pollutants that make it into their soils affect their crops. They do not have the sort of buffer that richer farmers have, and so they face starvation as a direct consequence of environmental devastation.

The problem is compounded because the poor do not have the luxury of long-term planning. Famine "leads them (and their animals) to assault the environment for short-term gains in ways they would never do if their incomes were stable above the subsistence level."[5] John M. Mellor, in an article for *Environment* magazine, notes that food scarcity's impact on the poor is especially acute because of the poor's inability to purchase available grain.[6]

The poor are impacted in two additional ways by environmental devastation. First, such problems as the destruction of the ozone layer, the greenhouse effect and pollution are mostly a consequence of Western abuses. The impact of Western lifestyles is global; hence, the poor suffer. Additionally, several Western corporations engage in direct destruction of the poor by shipping harmful waste products to their territories for disposal and by selling them pesticides and other chemicals that have been banned in the United States because of their danger to humans.

A Sudanese agronomist, Arif Jamal, recounted to the United Nations the decimation of animals caused by the distribution of barrels of pesticide that specifically state that they are not authorized for use in the States. "Where is the morality?" Jamal correctly asks.[7]

Jamal revealed that barrels of concentrated DDT (manufactured in Delaware but not for sale in the United States) had killed buffalo, gazelles, lions and birds in the Sudan. To make matters worse, the poisoned animals were skinned, and their meat was sold in markets.

One common factor in poverty is illiteracy, and the poor suffer additionally from not being able to read warning signs (written in English) that would steer them away from dangerous pesticides. They also suffer from improper use of the chemicals because of their inability to follow technical directions in English.

A total of 500 million pounds of chemicals banned in the United States are exported to Third World nations each year. The World Health Organization estimates that as many as one million people are acutely poisoned each year by these chemicals and that 20,000 die as a direct consequence of exposure.[8]

In addition to selling these poisonous chemicals to the poor, Western countries are paying poor governments to accept their toxic wastes. A Philadelphia firm recently contracted a Norwegian firm to dispose of 15,000 tons of toxic material on Kssa (a resort island off Guinea). An Italian firm dumped 10,000 barrels of toxic waste in the small Nigerian town of Koko for a lot fee of $100 per month. In 1988, Guinea-Bissau signed a five-year contract to accept European industrial waste for $120 million a year—just under the nation's gross national product of $150 million. Development expert Pat Costner says, "By allowing waste exports, industrialized countries are forcing developing countries to choose between poverty and poison."[9]

Toxic Garbage

If we don't have enough love to treat our neighbors right, do we at least have enough sense to treat ourselves right? The answer, sadly, is too often no.

Toxic waste has become such a problem in the States that New York City, for example, has assembled a specialized twenty-two-person police unit whose only duty is to sniff out culprit dumpers.[10] Disposing of the city's waste had involved huge payoffs of up to $600,000 to landfill managers who allowed corporations to dump their toxic liquids at night.

By far the biggest culprit in the U.S. toxic-waste predicament is the military-industrial complex. According to a feature on radioactive waste in *Technology Review,* forty-five cents of every dollar spent to make bomb-grade material goes toward managing wastes—as much as $100 billion a year. That is not to say that the toxic waste is safely disposed of: "Billions of gallons of radioactive wastes . . . have been dumped directly into soil and groundwater. Millions more gallons of concentrated waste have been stored in tanks, many of which have leaked."[11]

Our expensive preoccupation with building bombs to protect us from the enemy is killing us.

Water

Water is involved in a continuous cycle. It gathers from underground into lakes and oceans and forests, where it evaporates or transpires (goes up through the trees into the sky). In the sky it collects into rain clouds, precipitates, and returns to the earth as rain or snow. It seeps down through the soil, gathers from underground into lakes . . . and so the cycle continues.

In the ground, water picks up improperly disposed toxic wastes. Additional pollution collects from sewage, drainage pipes, and pesticides or fertilizers that collect in run-off water. Even underground fuel-storage tanks develop leaks, contaminating such famous pure-water sources as Arrowhead Springs.

In less developed and poorer countries, where sewer treatment is rare, water pollution is particularly acute and disease is rampant. Millions of children's deaths could be prevented each year through the implementation of very simple sanitation measures. Diseases that have been completely eradicated in the West for some time are present in these less developed countries solely because of inadequate sanitation.[12]

Drinkable water is only 1 per cent of the total world supply of water. That minuscule percentage is, of course, replenished through the cycle, but large quantities—exactly how much has not yet been determined—are lost to run-off in the ocean and to toxic contamination. Water consumption has increased dramatically over the past thirty years, and the average North American is a major factor in that increase. We consume, for example, seventy times more water per day than the average Ghanaian.

It is fair to say that water is scarce. In the future it will become more of a bargaining chip and power lever. In such struggles, the poor are the most likely to lose. Sandra Pastel, in *Worldwatch*, suggests that "water security" will have no winners unless societies can recognize the limited freshwater resources and "bring human numbers and wants into line" with those limits.[13]

Deforestation, God's Creatures and (Gasp!) Air
Imagine standing in a central park in Mexico City and being struck by a bird falling out of the sky—dead. It happens. Toxic air poisons

the bird and it falls, gasping, to earth.

The whole planet is gasping. A combination of tree-cutting and the releasing of chlorofluorocarbons is choking the earth—and thousands of species along with it—to death.

The primary cause of our current imbalance is deforestation. God created trees to interact with human respiration. We take in the oxygen plants give off, they take in the carbon dioxide we give off. A sort of global balancing act of inhaling and exhaling keeps the planet rocking. Yet at least twenty-seven million acres of tropical forests—the "lungs" of the globe—are being destroyed per year. The Amazon Basin, the primary rain forest in this breathing system, has already been destroyed by 20 per cent. Less carbon dioxide is being absorbed because of fewer trees, which means excess carbon dioxide in the air. And the world gets less rain, because fewer trees means less transpiration. The effects are felt around the world. Ethiopia's drought has been in part a consequence of tree-slashing in Brazil. (Transpiration from Amazon trees is the primary source of rain clouds all the way across the ocean in North Africa.) China has not been replacing the vast numbers of trees it cuts and consequently is vulnerable to mudslides and devastating floods. Japan's building industry has produced a high lumber demand. Major logging contracts have been written up with Thailand, Indonesia, the Philippines and Papua New Guinea. As a consequence, all these countries are now suffering from deforestation.

Central America has been quietly destroying its forests at a rate ten times greater than Brazil's. El Salvador has been bombing and burning its forests in search of rebels, and Guatemala has been using the defoliation approach the United States used in Vietnam in pursuit of rebel units.[14] Cambodia has been seeking to pay off its creditors with logs rather than hard currency; countries that need the lumber, such as neighboring Thailand, have been quick to go along with the scheme. At this point Cambodia is still 70 per cent covered by forest and could interrupt a dangerous course of action.[15]

Once again, the issue of poverty is raised when one considers the deforestation problem. Heavy indebtedness to developed nations makes trees a welcome source of revenue for Third World governments. And Western governments and corporations willing to accept debt repayments from logging revenues are culpable. The world is an interrelated mix of economies and environment; no business happens in a vacuum free of these problems. To engage in international business is to accept partnership in the world's system. Can the hand say to the lung, "I don't need you"?

Sadly, just as the poor come out on the bottom of the environmental mess, so do thousands of species that are dependent on rain forests for their survival. A majority of all the world's species live exclusively in the rain forests.[16] Deforestation, however, is contributing to the total extinction of more than 1,000 species per year.[17] To return to an earlier analogy, we're stomping on special creations on the living-room floor.

Finally, consider the ozone and the greenhouse effect. These are more difficult concepts to grasp, but two basic facts are clear. One, we are protected from the sun's ultraviolet radiation because of a sort of shroud around the earth called the ozone layer. Chlorofluorocarbons (CFCs) destroy that protective ozone shield. The sources of CFCs include air conditioning, agents used in making foam, and aerosol spray cans (such as those used for deodorant). So many CFCs have made it into the atmosphere that a hole the size of the United States has appeared in the ozone layer over Antarctica. Fortunately, few people live there. But what if the hole expands to cover the populated continents? There will be, at the least, an epidemic of cancer.

Second, the greenhouse effect is connected to the destruction of rain forests. Because there are fewer trees, unusually high amounts of carbon dioxide remain in the atmosphere. Heat given off by the earth usually escapes through the atmosphere into space, but carbon dioxide absorbs heat and keeps it within the earth's atmosphere. A possible consequence is increased temperatures; the eventual result, prominent scientists warn, could be a melting of the polar ice caps, causing floods on most of the world's shores and the jeopardizing of plant life. The consequences of that, of course, would eventually be mass starvation.

Restoring Our Love

On one hand, caring for creation can appear too daunting a task, one that involves corporations and governments across the ocean. What's one person to do? Yet caring for the environment requires that each of us do his or her part. Tasks such as recycling, conserving water, carpooling and walking, and being careful with energy consumption are all significant steps in the right direction.

Writer Ruth Goring Stewart sums up the Christian posture before the creation this way: "We are to *use* the creation; we are to *serve* and *tend* it; we are to *celebrate* it; and we are to *listen* to it."[18] Her book, *Environmental Stewardship* (InterVarsity Press, 1990), has a fine resource list at the end for practical steps to take in assuming care of the environment.

"The earth is the LORD's, and everything in it" (Ps 24:1; 1 Cor 10:26). We are invited to explore the splendor of God's creation and to care for it gently. In doing so, we'll discover that it whispers back to us the character of God and sings *with* us in praise to the Creator. By God's mercy we will find ourselves *restored* to creation, rather than persisting in the arrogant independence that has too long characterized humanity's relationship with God's handiwork.

Ecostatistics

The typical American discards 590 kilograms (1,300 pounds) of garbage a year *(Time).*

In one year, the average American
- discards 38 kilograms (84 pounds) of plastic;
- uses 140,000 liters (37,000 gallons) of water;
- eats more than 50 kilograms (110 pounds) of meat;
- uses 1,125 liters (300 gallons) of gasoline *(Time).*

Enough dirty diapers are dumped in the United States each year to stretch to the moon and back seven times *(Omni).*

For each ton of paper recycled, 3,700 pounds of lumber and 24,000 gallons of water are saved *(Omni).*

If the United States recycled half of the newspapers it discards every year, 6 million tons of waste would never reach landfills, and 3,200 garbage trucks that normally haul trash to the dump daily would stay idle *(Omni).*

Every hour Americans go through 2.5 million plastic beverage bottles *(Omni).*

We throw away enough glass every two weeks to fill the World Trade Center's 1,377-foot-tall twin towers *(Omni).*

Each year the amount of energy that leaks through American windows equals the amount of oil that flows through the Alaskan pipeline *(Omni).*

The U.S. government estimates that it will cost $100-200 billion just to clean up national defense wastes at Department of Energy facilities, not including the hazardous chemical and radioactive waste at facilities operated by the Department of Defense *(USA Today).*

Acid rain causes an estimated $5 billion of damage a year to buildings and other structures in seventeen Northeastern and Midwestern states *(National Wildlife).*

Estimated global pesticide sales in 1975: $5 billion. Projected for 1990: $50 billion *(National Wildlife).*

Number of dusky seaside sparrows in 1970: about 1,000. In 1989: 0 *(National Wildlife).*

Estimated number of African elephants in 1970: 4.5 million. In 1989: 500,000-650,000 *(National Wildlife).*

5

Setting the Captives Free

When I utter the splendid word freedom, *I utter it with all the love and fervor in my heart.*
POPE JOHN PAUL IN CZECHOSLOVAKIA, APRIL 1, 1990

THE years 1989-1990 will be recorded by historians as the time of the Great Global Democratic Revolution—that period when millions across the globe walked into the kings' palaces, stormed the presidents' residences, and defied the military establishments' tanks. Their dreams of toppling government and letting the people rule was the stuff that revolutions were made of.

In the Philippines, a senator's wife peacefully wrested power from the richest Third World despot. In Pakistan, a rebel president's daughter rose to victory through an election upset. A publisher beat Marxism at the Nicaraguan polls. A poet and playwright became president of Czechoslovakia, a union leader helped to oust the communists in Poland, and a pastor sparked the revolution in

Romania. None of these unlikely leaders claimed experience, competence or politico-economic savvy; rather, they offered the possibility of freedom.

Freedom never comes without a price, however. And now, as more than forty liberation movements sweep the globe, thousands are counting the cost.

In Asia, several hundred thousands have been killed and millions have been displaced. In the Indian state of Punjab, Sikhs have been fighting for more than six years for their own state. Just north of them, separatist Muslims in the Jammu and Kashmir states are fighting for their own country. In the same region, the Indian government is locked in an uneasy standoff with Pakistani soldiers who are challenging the border between the two nations. On the small island of Sri Lanka, thousands have been killed through torture and burning, more than 10,000 are in prison, up to forty political killings occur every day, and inflation is up to fifty per cent.[1]

In Myanmar (formerly Burma), opium finances an estimated 16,000 Shan guerrillas.[2] Tibet declared its independence from China in 1989, to which the government responded with the imprisonment of over 1,000 leaders, re-education camps, and restricted religious practices. China brutally suppressed that country's student-led call for democratic reforms in the summer of 1989. Kampuchea, Malaysia, Laos, Vietnam, Afghanistan, North and South Korea, Thailand, the Philippines and Indonesia are embroiled in liberation conflicts. (Meanwhile, almost unnoticed, Taiwan moved toward democracy with a multiparty election on December 2, 1989).

In Latin America, where rising poverty often stresses the limits of governments, liberation movements have added to the misery. Right-wing governments and left-wing guerrillas have been responsible for the deaths of more than 100,000 civilians in Guatemala and El Salvador, where both nationalistic and Marxist elements have been fighting for freedom. *Contras* killed as many as 30,000 Nicaraguans in the ten-year battle to oust the Marxist government. Peru continues to suffer from attacks by the *Sendero Luminoso,* a Maoist guerrilla organization responsible for several thousand deaths in 1989 alone. Unlike other liberation groups in Latin America, the *Sendero Luminoso* does not appear to have significant indigenous support, nor does it seek to build bridges with communities that could further its cause. In 1989 this group assassinated thirty-two mayors.

The Horn of Africa is a caldron of bloody conflicts and starvation. There, the three bordering nations of Ethiopia, Somalia and Sudan are tangled in a mess of civil and national wars exacerbated by years of severe drought.

Neighboring Sudan is no stranger to conflict. Its own battle for independence from Britain cost it more than 500,000 lives. And now as many as 250,000 have died in its own civil war, waged mostly in the south between Christian and animist factions that have resisted the Muslim government and its required adherence to Islamic law since 1983. The cost in human lives of this war has been so severe that in 1989 the military ousted the democratically elected government and vowed to remove the Islamic restrictions. Even so, two-thirds of all Sudanese are Muslims; the future will not be simple.

Meanwhile, Somalia, on Ethiopia's eastern border, is locked in a civil war that has killed thousands and mobilized a refugee population of more than 300,000 who have fled into Ethiopia. That people are migrating to Ethiopia—a nation beset with famine, civil war and pestilence—indicates the seriousness of Somalia's conflict.

Europe, of course, is exploding with liberation and has significantly shifted the complexion of freedom fighters. Mikhail Gorbachev is the unquestioned champion of this phenomenon, and now the train that he pushed over the top of the hill has taken on its own momentum and is outpacing his ability to lead. Not only have European liberation movements resulted in every satellite Eastern European nation's rejection of Moscow's rule, but already three provinces of the USSR—Lithuania, Latvia and Estonia, which border the other Eastern European nations—have declared independence.

Western stereotypes of democracy are being challenged by these emerging governments: the Berlin Wall was peacefully removed by those whom many called "enemies." To further twist the frame of reference of North Americans, Gorbachev was waging peace throughout the communist world while the United States invaded Panama.

Perhaps the single greatest outcome of this current movement toward liberation is the willingness of old enemies to talk. President Bush telephones Mikhail Gorbachev; François Mitterand and Helmut Kohl ask Lithuania to talk with Moscow; and South Africa's Frederick de Klerk begins his own talks with the previously imprisoned Nelson Mandela and the previously banned African National Congress. We can hope, too, that the influence of Gorbachev and Eastern Europe will spill over into Northern Ireland.

The Various Faces of Liberation

Although liberation movements grow out of similar states of oppression and share similar goals for the future, they by no means all look alike. Liberation movements profoundly reflect the cultural histories and religious convictions of the nations and people involved. Consider, for example, the following thumbnail histories of liberation movements in Latin America and Africa.

Latin America's liberation movements have been church-based, heavily influenced by Catholicism. The Roman Catholic "base communities" have served as centers of discussion and strategic planning where local priests have preached the biblical standards of justice and dignity. What could best be described as a continent-wide movement in the 1970s, liberation theology flourished in these communities with a call to stand up and demand justice for the poor and, if necessary, face the brutal repression of governments. Liberation theology was expressed in a variety of forms, from nonviolent activism to aggressive military action.

On the other hand, Africa's liberation movements have largely addressed the wrongs of Western colonialism. From the mid-1600s to the late 1800s, Africa was a battleground of Western powers scrambling for their share of that unexplored pie. The chief villains were the British, French, Portuguese, Spanish, Belgians and Dutch. Africa became both a resource for cheap labor and minerals and a land mass for the extension of empires. Cecil John Rhodes of Britain was most articulate in this regard when he proclaimed the throne's desire to fly its flag all the way from Cape Town to Cairo. Blacks became the victims, not only of these territorial visions but also of the economic deprivation that resulted from the extraction of valuable natural resources. And of course, hundreds of thousands of Blacks were killed in the intercolonial wars that took place on African soil. In response, liberation movements were born. In 1957, Nigeria led the way in demanding independence from its colonial oppressor. Since then every political state fashioned by colonial power, excepting South Africa, has gained independence. Thus Africa today is a collection of over forty experimental governments with an average age of less than twenty years.

Understanding Liberation
Dom Helder Camara, a church leader in Central America, said,

"When I give food to the poor, they call me a saint. When I ask *why* the poor have no food, they call me a communist."

Liberation movements are mostly a response to structural injustice. People with power have organized a system of control that oppressses others. Sometimes that system is mobilized to exert its control far beyond national borders. Hitler is an obvious example, but most oppressive systems are confined within national borders.

Unfortunately, few structural injustices are clearly defined, and too often people are swayed by political interest groups rather than biblical sensibilities in the face of the messy world of liberation. The larger Cold War has been a convenient medium for politicians to mask the true nature of several of the world's liberation movements.

In Nicaragua, for example, the Sandinistas came to power after a prolonged battle with dictator Anastasio Somoza, whose greed had deeded him virtually the entire fishing and shipping industry of his nation and up to a third of the land. A spectrum of "freedom fighters" ousted him—with the blessing of the United States. However, the new ruling junta included members with Marxist leanings, and the Carter administration protested by withdrawing financial aid. Nicaragua then went hunting for alternative sources of income and found a friend in the Soviet Union. One year later, President Reagan began to describe Nicaragua as a Marxist nation and assembled and funded a guerrilla force, known as *contras,* to overthrow the Sandinista government. Nicaragua, a little country whose population was less than that of the city of Los Angeles, was now fighting the world's greatest military power. More funds were required from the Soviets, and this served as further "proof" of Nicaragua's Marxist leanings.

Eventually, a ravaged economy led to dialog with the opposition, and a peaceful election transpired; the opposition party won. Violeta Chamorro, the new president, immediately appointed the Sandinistas' four-star general Humberto Ortega to head her military. United States leaders were dismayed once again, and an undersecretary for Latin American affairs was sent to Chamorro with the message that financial aid was in jeopardy as long as Ortega remained on board.

What our nation failed to realize was that poverty and Western-sponsored oppression—not Marxism—brought the Sandinistas to power. Many of the world's liberation movements have simply found "Marxism" a handy title to slap on their causes, because of Marxism's original aspirations of representing the oppressed. Sadly, our misrepresentation of the causes of revolutionary uprisings has resulted in violence being returned for violence. In El Salvador, the U.S. government spends one million dollars per day to arm a government that has killed 70,000 of its citizens—in the name of protecting those citizens from Marxism. Recently those arms were used to kill six Jesuit priests and two of their staff. Two of the soldiers who did the killing had graduated just two days earlier from a U.S. military school.

Structural injustice can also be expressed in the form of robbing people of their cultural heritage and dignity. The Soviet Union is currently struggling with the consequences of this. The three western provinces that have just declared independence did so to the tunes of their old national anthems. The people garbed themselves in traditional dress and spontaneously joined in folk dances. These people face tremendous economic hardship because of their declarations, but they feel that it would be better to have death than no dignity.

When the United Nations was founded in 1945, it declared that one-third of the world's population was best described as ethnic societies controlled by colonial governments. The agenda was set to move these 750 million people toward self-government. Today fewer than one million of those originally listed remain under the control of colonial powers. This tremendous success notwithstanding, what has emerged since is the realization that the wolves had defined the rules for the sheep. Millions more people were left under the control of colonial powers because the top-ranking members of the United Nations considered their own "security interests" more important than those ethnic groups' independence. Lithuania, Latvia and Estonia are cases in point. Ethnic-based liberation movements will dominate the agendas of world leaders in the decade ahead.

The world is divided into 226-plus political entities, yet at least twice that number of sizable ethnic groups exist. When these are broken into smaller units, some ethnologists count as many as 26,000 peoples. There is no ethnically pure nation in the world today, but some ethnic groups have clearly dominated, and in some instances nearly exterminated, other ethnic populations in the formation of political entities. To stir the stew even more, at least 77 ethnic groups (of the world's 575) are settled *across* national boundaries. The Tamils, for example, spread from southern India to northern Sri Lanka. Lebanon is the most poignant example of a country that could not resolve internal ethnic tensions. The challenge faced by young Third World and Eastern European governments will be to create nation-states that elevate the value of cultural diversity and dependency. Neither full independence from the government nor full integration into society will be an option for these ethnic groups.[3] "Remembering the past is a political act."[4] Herein lies much of the energy for current liberation movements. Poles remember the 1.8 million relatives transported to Siberia; Czechs remember the 1968 Soviet invasion; Romanians remember the 60,000 citizens killed under Ceausescu; Germans remember August 13, 1961, when barbed wire (soon to be the Berlin Wall) suddenly separated family members; White Afrikaners remember the deaths of 28,000 women and children in British concentration camps at the turn of the century; and Jews in Israel remember smokestacks throughout Europe in the 1940s.

When wars are "won" by the stronger of two sides, a history of the fighting nations is inevitably recorded by the victor—most often as a means to justify the violence committed in the name of higher purposes. The defeated, however, find their own means of passing down their versions of history, and these stories eventually become the poetry of rebellions.

Perhaps the two most important questions one can ask in order to understand a liberation movement are: What structures are destroying these people? and What do these people remember about the past? These powerful questions are linked to no particular political orientation and bring as much moral clarity when answered by Native Americans in the United States as when they are answered by Poles in Eastern Europe.

Tomorrow's Hot Spots

No one can predict future revolutions with certainty, yet several liberation movements that are currently rumbling will surely take significant turns in the decade ahead.

China's leadership has meticulously yet unwittingly laid the groundwork for today's youth to ask tomorrow's revolutionary question: Do you remember Tiananmen Square? The horrifying sound of skulls being run over by tanks, the images of machine guns fired point-blank in the faces of thousands of unarmed civilians, the stories of lobotomies performed on student leaders, and the unabashed denial by the Chinese government that any such atrocities occurred—all have secured the future liberation movement in China as a fact. Every night hundreds of thousands of Chinese, in the privacy of homes and dormitory rooms, recount the stories that will become tomorrow's ballads. Around the world some 500,000 Chinese students are pursuing their studies of government, law and economics with a greater sense of purpose, as they now perceive their academic load as revolutionary mortar.

The media coverage of the Beijing massacre, the concurrent demise of the first great communist empire and its satellite states, and the unified international outrage against Deng's actions make the liberation movement irreversible. The "Goddess of Democracy" originally erected in Tiananmen Square has become an international symbol of this coming movement. Already dozens of replicas have adorned city squares around the world, miniature versions sit on thousands of shelves and dangle on key rings, and a ship by the same name hopes to sit off the coast of China and beam prodemocracy messages into that nation.

What will emerge is not clear. Democratic reforms will lead the way, but as with the Soviet Union, *perestroika* and *glasnost* will unleash other questions of the past and ethnic rivalries that have been suppressed by the current government. The reports of China's rapidly growing church will finally open themselves to Western investigation, and the spiritual questions resulting from the void created by a failed materialistic model of life will give new opportunity for the sharing of Christian faith. Communism as a *global phenomenon* will breathe its last.

Of particular concern in the coming decade will be the Soviet-controlled Islamic regions of the USSR, which account for 20 per cent of that nation's population. The bordering nations of Iran, Afghanistan and Pakistan, which are virtually 100 per cent Islamic, ensure a base of operation for freedom fighters—with printing presses at their disposal—who do remember the past and who are inspired by the vision of a society run wholly in submission to Allah.

The liberation movement in South Africa will finally achieve its goal of a democratic society. In a very real sense, all of Africa waits and groans for its freedom. The last of Africa's countries to be ruled by a colonially installed government, South Africa will undergo a liberation that will signify the final liberation of all of Black Africa. In a sense, the continent will "come of age" and will experience a fresh vision and renewed commitment to unity in the face of such internal difficulties as ethnic strife and poverty.

South Africa's struggle is an important point of reflection for Western Christians. While the ravages of communism are easily explained away as the logical extension of godless systems, South Africa's horrendous system of oppression was designed, implemented and morally defended by the country's White-run church. The African National Congress, formed in 1912 with the simple goal of a democratic society for all races, was denied its vision by the British, the Afrikaners and several Western nations (including the United States). Power was automatically and always left with the Whites, whose decisions were made without question.

If China's liberation will reflect the demise of communism and *atheistic* government, and South Africa's liberation will reflect the disgrace of *Christianity* married to political aspirations and ethnic pride, Israel's woes will reflect *Judaism's* total break with the Old Testament Yahweh and his call to do justice to all peoples.

The intransigent posture of Israel's conservative Likud Party has galvanized international opinion against Israel. More than 130 Palestinian villages have been demolished by Israel's troops; more than 6,000 Palestinian youth are currently in Israel's prisons—no charges given. Schools have been closed, freedom of press denied, taxation without representation imposed and severe mobility restrictions enforced. In these ways, at least, Israel is the South Africa of the Middle East.

Hundreds of children have been killed by police bullets during the past two years, and, once again, stories are being told around dinner tables and in playgrounds that will eventually become the poetry of liberation. Each Palestinian funeral is laying the foundation for the revolutionary question "Do you remember the past?"

As the international Christian community is faced with this violence, it is also confronted with Jesus' words that accused Israel's leaders of New Testament days of focusing on outward forms of religion while forsaking the "weightier matters of the law"—that is, doing justice and loving mercy.

Sensationalist end-times books and movies in the 1970s blinded the Western church to the demand for justice in Israel, calling Christians to defend Israel's territorial existence as the highest good. Godless communism was supposed to sweep down on Israel and attempt to obliterate it. Western champions of democracy and God would thwart that evil intent, Armageddon would ensue, and Jesus would return. With godless communism almost out of the picture now, perhaps Christians will be able to turn their focus back to the Scriptures' call to righteous living as the standard by which Israel's actions must be judged.

Taking Action for Tomorrow

Those of us who are serious in our desire to engage tomorrow's world with God's love will first of all need to be convinced of the biblical call to *do justice*.

At a political level, liberation movements will require us to be bigger people than our nation's political leaders. The convenient categories of "Democrat" and "Republican" simply do not carry a noble enough vision of what God intends for the nations. The emerging evangelical global activist will aspire to a much more profound understanding of political reality and the gospel's demands for just government.

These liberation movements will also call us to use our minds. *Understanding* the abuses that make up the history of oppressed peoples will be critical to our ability to effectively serve others who live in societies going through the fearful and exciting changes of liberation. The Western church's ignorance of the facts in South Africa is one good contemporary example of our failure in this regard.

We will also have to confront the question of violence. Christian leaders have uncritically supported the call to arms on both sides of liberation struggles. More than 80 per cent of the fatalities in current liberation movements are civilians—women and children who had no say in the violence. In the days to come, Christians who call for a laying down of arms, without regard for whose political interests are being served, will be in the forefront of the greatest liberation movement—God's call to be peacemakers.

Finally, Western Christians who commit themselves to care for a globe tangled in the mess of liberation wars will begin to address the serious abuses of our own history—the near genocide of Native Americans, the evil treatment of African-Americans, and the abuse of Mexican-Americans. Justice is a two-edged sword: When we wield it against the evil structures in the world, it cuts back into the evil structures we ourselves have built and now maintain. Ultimately, our only moral license to denounce structural injustice of any sort, be it communism or right-wing apartheid, is our personal repentance for complicity in the evil structures in our own land. Anything less would be hypocrisy.

chapter **6**

The Urban
Challenge

IMAGES of urban squalor and human suffering are not in short supply. I heard my first church lecture on the city when I was seven years old. The story was of a young woman living in New York City. She was apparently stabbed to death while screaming for help to hundreds of onlookers who didn't so much as call the police. I remember thinking that New York must be a terrible place to live. It took me several years to unlearn that urban stereotype.

Whatever our image of the city, we need to become acquainted with it; soon, most of us will be living there. In 1800, just 2.4 per cent of the world's population lived in cities. Two hundred years later, in 1990, 47 per cent of the world live in urban areas. And the move to the city is not slowing down.

Every day, Mexico City and Bombay add 3,000 new residents. Sao Paulo grows by almost 2,000 per day, as do Shanghai, Beijing and Calcutta. In 1900, only one city boasted a population of five million—London. Today, more than forty cities are that populous; within one generation, forty-seven cities will have grown beyond ten million residents, with Mexico City and Shanghai both over thirty-six million. People who love others and who desire meaningful ministry will want to understand the soul of the city.

What Is a City?

In its simplest definition, the city is just a well-organized collection of services that benefit its residents—transportation, sewer systems, judicial courts, grocery stores, schools, hospitals and the arts. Businesses cluster together because of the benefits of mass production, communication, expertise and available labor. Cities are able to thrive because necessary energy and food supplies are supplied en masse. On the eve of the Industrial Revolution only 3 per cent of the world was urban. The ability to harness fossil fuels played a chief role in the ushering in of the revolution and the sudden growth of cities. Fuels provided the necessary energy for industry and housing but also increased agricultural yields (through fertilizers), and thus the city's laborers were able to live without growing their own food.[1] Industrial laborers became specialized, and productivity and services increased.

But the city is much more than organized services. It is the town square where opinions are expressed and passions vented. For example, a million demonstrators flooded the streets of Manila, Philippines, to peacefully overthrow dictator Ferdinand Marcos. Since then, national capitals have become the heart of liberation movements, and the mention of their names conjures up the revolutions of 1989-1990: Beijing, Bucharest, Prague, Berlin, Warsaw,

Budapest, Timisoara, Vilnius, Seoul, Soweto, Managua, Panama City.

In my city, Los Angeles, 500,000 Hispanics showed up this year to celebrate Cinco de Mayo in an unprecedented show of Latino solidarity. London's Wimbledon Stadium packed in 72,000 youths to welcome Soweto's Nelson Mandela. Washington, D.C., received 350,000 demonstrators to protest abortion restrictions, and a few months later 250,000 streamed in to call for greater abortion restrictions.

In the decade ahead, we'll learn the names of dozens more town squares around the world. Politicians, poets, rock musicians, preachers and laborers will assemble in greater numbers than ever before in the history of the world both to demand their rights and to celebrate their freedoms. One day the world will watch the live broadcast of three million jubilant Chinese dancing in Tiananmen Square and the surrounding area. And those of us who watched the government slaughter of 1989 will join in the dance, as our living rooms and barrooms become extensions of China's town square. The media have given us a town square the size of the world.

United in Diversity

The city is also a place of *diversity.* Mexico City holds more members of each of Mexico's indigenous peoples than the villages themselves hold. Toronto, Canada, is 70 per cent ethnic, and the United Nations calls it the most international gathering place on earth. Los Angeles, California, is home to more than 100 first-generation language groups; Hollywood High School offers classes in thirty-six of those languages. In fact, Los Angeles is the world's second-largest Vietnamese city, Mexican city, Filipino city, Guatemalan city, Salvadoran city and Korean city.

Fundamentally, this diversity enriches the city. God's fabulous creation is experienced in much greater degree amid such varied strains of color and culture. Customs, foods, dress, music, histories, holidays and recreation are ours for the choosing. Systems that suppress such diversity, such as South Africa's apartheid government, leave people culturally "undernourished," as if they were being fed a steady diet of just one of the major food groups.

This diversity also brings a broader tolerance of others and their values. Whereas one's convictions or assumptions can go unchallenged in an isolated village or farm community, the city models just about every value *in the public forum,* and people are much freer to make their own decisions. This freedom challenges our stereotypes of other peoples and religions; it calls Christians to *live* their faith in public, not just talk about it.

Bright Lights, Big Problems

Exploitation, crime, disease, hunger, homelessness and unemployment greet millions of new arrivals who come to the city in search of a better economic future. According to one expert, by the year 2000 more than two billion people will live in underdeveloped cities, and of that number, 846 million will live as squatters—virtual refugees locked into despair and disease.[2] In Nairobi and Manila, half the residents live in slums; in Calcutta, 70 per cent.[3] Many cities of the world are simply unable to sustain adequate services, given their rapid growth. Consequently, the cycle of poverty—and its associated problems—becomes a widening spiral. Unemployment leads to poor housing and crime, which leads to disease, violence and death. Committed teachers are rare in such environments—which leads to substandard education, illiteracy, and, once again, unemployment.

Just correcting *one* of these variables is no easy task. For example, were Sao Paulo to upgrade its sanitation to European standards—providing clean running water and sewage systems—it would require the city's entire budget for thirty years.[4] Up to 60 per cent of Calcutta's population suffers from breathing disorders due to smog.[5] Malaria and cholera are a way of life for Nairobi's 500,000 slum residents; poverty-driven prostitution contributes to the spread of AIDS in the same slums, where 6,000 documented cases raise questions about the number of undocumented cases.[6] More than 1.2 million slum dwellers live in Bangkok, a city of six million, where human excrement, rats, stagnant water and trash line the alleyways that serve as children's playgrounds. In Cairo, a city of fifteen million, 60 per cent of the population lives below the poverty line. Bangkok and Bombay are home to 500,000 and 300,000 child prostitutes, respectively.

A city's most vulnerable spot is its dependence on outside sources of food and energy. When shortages prevail, the poor are hardest hit. The price of fresh vegetables goes up due to a crop failure and the poor resort to a higher-carbohydrate diet, unable to afford the new prices. Body resistance is lowered and sickness becomes acute. Doctors' fees cannot be paid so misery increases and the ailments spread. Likewise, rising kerosene prices mean less heat, which translates to debilitating fevers and death in winter.

Sadly, children are the most numerous victims of the city's poverty. Some 40 per cent of the world's slum dwellers are under fifteen years old. More than 100 million of these children lead their own lives, entirely without adult connection, and their homes are literally the sidewalks. They are the most susceptible to the extreme conditions of cold, homelessness, disease and poor nutrition. Brain damage and physical deformity almost guarantee a lifetime of misery for millions of the young. And of course, the young are vulnerable to forced child labor, prostitution and pornography. Some, for the sake of survival, join street gangs and eventually enter a lifestyle of crime and periodic imprisonment. Says Larry Wilson in *Childlife*, "To many, children growing up in Third-World cities are non-peoples. Lives with no voice. The powerless minority. They have no courts to appeal to, no representation in governments and are too small and weak to fight back."[7]

The fact of urban poverty makes concern for the city all the more acute for the Christian church, because Third World urban centers are the world's fastest-growing cities. By the year 2000, twelve of the world's largest fifteen cities will be Third World cities. It is estimated that from 1990 to 2025 (one generation) the number of developed nations' cities of larger than one million will have increased from 105 cities to 150; Third World cities of one million or more, on the other hand, will have increased from 120 to 500.

The Soul of the City

Finally, the city is a place of deep spiritual need and opportunity. Poverty inflicts immense wounds on the heart and the mind: prostitution, child labor, death, separation and fear leave scars that only the gospel can heal. It's as though God were speaking directly to these victims when he announced his coming in Isaiah 61:

The Spirit of the Sovereign LORD is on me,
   because the LORD has anointed me
   to preach good news to the poor.
He has sent me to bind up the brokenhearted,
   to proclaim freedom for the captives
   and release from darkness for the prisoners,
to proclaim the year of the LORD's favor
   and the day of vengeance of our God,
to comfort all who mourn,
   and provide for those who grieve in Zion—
to bestow on them a crown of beauty

    instead of ashes,
  the oil of gladness
    instead of mourning,
  and a garment of praise
    instead of a spirit of despair. (Is 61:1–3)

Nowhere has the gospel made more sense than in this context of total human pain. All of the good news comes alive as Christians minister to the whole person. We find ourselves not only address-ing the personal dimensions of pain but also confronting the struc-tural evil of the city, which is often the basis of personal pain.

For Christians to be effective in this environment will require a wholistic understanding of the purpose and substance of the gos-pel. Urban researcher Ray Bakke says, "Those who preach that we should only save souls, preach, and plant churches without getting involved socially in society are really doing two things: one, admit-ting to the irrelevance of the gospel over large sectors of modern life and, secondly, tacitly supporting the socially sinful status quo."[8]

The urban challenge is perhaps the most serious indictment of Western churches. In the United States the term "white flight" provides an accurate picture of how the church has left the ghetto. The goal of high property values and safe neighborhoods prompts more Christians to *leave* these places of pain than to minister in their midst. Which of these two actions embodies the heart of the gospel? One would expect the unredeemed person, not the re-deemed one, to run away from human suffering and despair.

It is not only a matter of spiritual principle. There is also the question of *personal* spiritual survival. Tony Campolo tells the sto-ry of a blond Californian who asked him if it would be dangerous to work in the ghettos of Philadelphia:

"Not half as dangerous as working in the affluent white suburbs where you're from," I responded after glancing at his application. He got my point—those who do not venture to serve the poor and wretched of the world may be very much in danger of neglecting experiences that can feed their souls and revitalize their spirits.

Those who can destroy the body, warned Jesus, are not half as dangerous as those who can destroy the soul. For many middle-class kids in suburban America there is not much of a physical threat to their well-being. There is immense spiritual threat, however. Living among the affluent and growing up on yuppie values can lead them into an insensitivity and egoism that spell spiritual death.[9]

The urban challenge is also a call back to the lifestyle of *incarnation.* The story of Jesus is the account of a spiritually powerful and wealthy person who gave it all up to walk among the harassed and helpless in weakness and vulnerability. It is impossible to minister fully to the urban person from big churches and mission headquarters that are safely located in the suburbs. Just as the "Word became flesh and made his dwelling among us" (Jn 1:14), so, too, we the body of Christ in today's society must live among the people we serve.

In my neighborhood, unemployment is high, drug abuse and crime are rampant, single-parent families are the norm, and police sirens, ambulances and ice-cream trucks compete for air time. Arrests are almost a daily occurrence; gunfire is part of the background noise at bedtime. I have watched well-meaning folk from nearby congregations come and do their weekend plunge in our neighborhood (70 per cent Black, 30 per cent Hispanic). If that is where they leave it, they might as well be door-to-door salespeople peddling products that have no connection to the real circumstances of inner-city living. At least some of these Christians need to live with the people to whom their church would minister.

It is one thing for a suburban witness team to "hit" the city with the gospel and "run" back home to the suburbs. It is something quite different to commit yourself to living a Christian witness in the city day in and day out. Ministry in urban centers requires that we become vulnerable to the daily life of city living, that we allow the gospel to work on our behalf. Out of that experience and understanding we will be equipped and empowered to serve our neighbors.

God's Will for the City

Ministry in the city also requires at least one biblical corrective. The squalor and evil that make up so much of life in the city have influenced Christian leaders to write off the city as a place reserved for God's judgment. Besides lacking the faith and compassion to believe that God can minister his mercy and healing in that environment, these leaders equate the city with the devil.

Jonah had the same problem. He was sent to Nineveh to call for repentance, to prevent God's judgment. But Jonah preferred God's judgment. The Scriptures tell us that Jonah sulked and was angry with God for redeeming that wicked urban center.

Nineveh's redemption was apparently so complete that Jesus warned the Pharisees that they would one day be judged by the Ninevites. Imagine the religious leaders of the day being judged by the inhabitants of what was once the most wretched of cities in recorded history. We must ask what Christ would say to us today with regard to our lifestyle and attitude toward the city.

The Bible calls us to seek the welfare of the city, to be a light in dark places, to be salt and preserve against decay. I hope that future generations of evangelicals will evidence such a deep love of God that they will find themselves drawn to urban centers of pain, where God can minister his tenderness and mercy to the poorest of the poor through them.

chapter 7

The Gorbachev Revolution

We have abandoned the claim to have a monopoly on the truth; we no longer think that we are always right, that those who disagree with us are our enemies. We have now decided, firmly and irrevocably, to base our policies on the principles of freedom of choice, and to develop our culture through dialogue and acceptance of all that is applicable in our conditions.[1]
MIKHAIL GORBACHEV ON COMMUNISM

We need spiritual values, we need a revolution of the mind. This is the only way toward a new culture and new politics that can meet the challenge of our time. We have changed our attitude toward some matters—such as religion—which, admittedly, we used to treat in a simplistic manner. . . . Now we not only proceed from the assumption that no one should interfere in matters of the individual's conscience; we also say that the moral values that religion generated and embodied for centuries can help in the work of renewal in our country, too.[2]
MIKHAIL GORBACHEV ON RELIGION

JOSEPH Stalin would have had him shot on the spot. Leonid Brezhnev probably would have been less violent, sentencing him to prison. Mikhail Gorbachev is neither speaking nor behaving like a communist. But does that mean he's *not* a communist? It's an interesting question. Communist by the classical definition? No. Communist by virtue of being president of the Soviet Union? Three years ago, that would have been a ridiculous question.

He's broken all the rules. Gorbachev has been retiring battalions, destroying warheads, retreating from invaded territories, slashing the military budget, and lecturing on the moral obligation of governments to stay out of the internal affairs of other nations. So stunning has been the transformation of Soviet leadership that the world's leading anti-Soviet spokesman, Ronald Reagan, told the world in a live broadcast from Red Square that the notion of the "evil empire" was a thing of the past. Gorbachev has dedicated himself to the dismantling of his empire.

A New Breeze
Because virtually no part of the world is unrelated to the Soviet Union, Gorbachev's revolution has sent everyone hopping—nations, presidents, politicians, the pope, Wall Street, academicians, musicians, economists, military alliances and church denominations. President Bush, caught off guard by news of the dismantled Berlin Wall, was so overwhelmed he couldn't answer reporters' questions. The "new breeze blowing," an image penned by the writer of Bush's inaugural speech, is a gale. And it's coming from the unlikeliest quarters.

Gorbachev has permanently altered global dynamics of politics and economics. The world is now a postcommunist society in the same sense that it became a post-Nazi society in 1945. The notion and threat of an international communist movement are dead. The romantic lure of a revolution that could turn nations over to the laborer, thereby allowing justice and dignity to prevail, proved false.

The Decline of Communism
Communism is now an Asian phenomenon. In North and South

America, the only real communist presence is Cuba; there the politics are best described as a personality government—a Fidel Castro dictatorship that probably will fall when he dies. Albania, the only remaining European communist nation, could be described similarly. Only three limping Marxist states stand among Africa's fifty countries, and their red colors are quickly fading. Ethiopia has been decimated by a combination of drought, mismanagement and civil war. Mozambique's Marxist revolution has failed. Its Marxist label is nothing more than that: a label. The country is essentially a fledgling Third World nation trying to establish itself after wresting control from its former colonial power, Portugal. Angola, the other African Marxist state, will—most likely—happily move from the Marxist camp when left to itself.

What began as a European movement has been abandoned by its grandchildren. With the loss of this link to the original sources, those few Asian countries holding on to Marxism have China as their stepparent—and China's Tiananmen Square massacre is the new history of Marxism. With all the world tuned in to those two brutal days, few will find Marxism an inspiring movement that comes *from* the people *for* the people. Indeed, the People's Republic of China is anything but "the people's." China now accounts for more than 90 per cent of the world's Marxist population, and its inevitable fall will leave a total global population of Marxists roughly equal to the population of Bangladesh.

Clearly, Gorbachev betrayed communism's founding fathers, and he never intended just a window-dressing job. In his own words, "After a mechanism has been tuned up, it gains a momentum of its own."[3] And again, *glasnost,* or "openness," is "an indispensable precondition for the democratization of society, one of the most important guarantees that the changes we have begun will be irreversible."[4] Gorbachev understood that his reforms were taking on the Bear. Gorbachev has opened his revolution to the world's press. The policy of *glasnost* has been his partner to ensure that people will have the opportunity once again to recall the past, which, as Gorbachev correctly understands, is one of the chief components of a liberation movement. *Glasnost* has challenged the unquestioned gods of Marxism, exposing the "holy temples" of the movement as being nothing more than places for uninhibited power orgies. *Glasnost* is the "re-evaluation of history."[5]

Gorbachev not only set *glasnost* in motion, he pushed Soviet allies to join him. He is the one who gave Milos Jakes of Czechoslovakia and Erich Honecker of East Germany the "thumbs down." In fact, Gorbachev warned that the Soviet empire would not lend military support to the lust that kept East German rulers in power, and he cautioned them that "life itself punishes those who delay." Poland's new president wishes him success, because his own liberation was enabled by Gorbachev. Of China's response to Tiananmen Square, Gorbachev said, "Not one Soviet, from the president down to a school child, approves of China's use of tanks to repress the students."[6]

God's Special Tool?

Perhaps we won't be sure of Gorbachev's motives until we get to heaven, but one has to wonder if he's the sort of king the Scriptures say God sovereignly establishes for the good of people. Indeed, the president of one of the largest and most politically conservative Christian organizations of the West told me that he considers Gorbachev God's special tool of the century to usher in an unprecedented harvest of evangelism.

Motives aside, what is clear is Gorbachev's enormous capacity to risk losing all power and position in pursuit of a higher good. Leaders have emerged in time of war to clamor for power over huge armies. Gorbachev, on the other hand, insists on clinging to a position of leadership that, by his own design, erodes with every passing minute. His success in battle is measured by the amount of territory he loses. It's the sort of upside-down kingdom approach you'd expect from Jesus' followers, and those of us from the West who have assumed that *our* political leaders were more likely to look like Jesus don't know what to do with Gorbachev.

Perhaps at the heart of his revolution is a genuine love for his country. The Soviet Union, though one of the two world superpowers, is declining to the status of an underdeveloped nation. Although Marxism guarantees every citizen a job and a good education, lack of adequate sanitation, medical care and nutritious meals is too much the norm for Soviet citizens. The Marxist ideal promised the best means to prosperity for the laborer. In fact, Nikita Khrushchev predicted that the day would come when Marxism would produce a wealthy society whose standard of living would parallel that of the United States. Yuri Andropov, one of Gorbachev's short-reigning predecessors, was so disturbed by the lack of economic progress in the Soviet model that he gave the call to the Central Committee to "find the answers." At the same time, China's Deng Xiaoping instituted economic reform at the local level that looked remarkably like free enterprise. His rationale was, "I don't care if a cat is black or white, as long as it catches mice." For Deng, "color" didn't mean power or no power; it meant slight adjustments to a system over which he and his politburo held absolute and unchallenged authority.

Nonetheless, Gorbachev surely was swayed by the questions of Andropov and Deng. Beyond that, his work as director of Soviet agriculture took him on tours of capitalistic nations where he encountered productivity, teamwork, high morale and a fairly high standard of living. These exposure trips forced questions into Gorbachev's mind. What emerged was a man much more *pragmatic* than *ideological* in his concern to provide for his people.

Gorbachev and *Glasnost*

Soviet leaders had always told their people that they were better off than capitalists. Gorbachev did what his predecessors did not— he told the truth. Soviet television and newspapers began to describe the reality of drug abuse, alcoholism, homelessness, prostitution, unemployment, sexually transmitted diseases and inflation.[7] Gorbachev's goal was two-pronged: put incentive for a better life back in the people's hands (the system couldn't do it) and sow discontent in the public's heart over the way things were, creating a grassroots level of support for reforms he would soon usher in. (Gorbachev installed Nobel Peace Prize winner Yevgeny Chazov as his minister of health, precisely because of Chazov's frank condemnation of Soviet health care.) Eastern Europe was quick to pick up the signals.

Gorbachev began to publish the statistics that indicated the Soviet Union's need for renewal: forty million Soviets (13 per cent of the population) lived below the poverty level; $70 billion was spent on the war in Afghanistan; the foreign trade deficit was $52 billion.[8] And he didn't promise any rose garden on the way to reform: sixteen million Soviets would be laid off from factory positions to trim the fat from state enterprises.[9] *Perestroika,* the restructuring of society that leads eventually to a healthy economy, was fraught with pain. The initial five years of this call for change has hurt the majority of laborers in the short run. This presents one of Gorbachev's most serious challenges: Will the people believe enough in him to go through the stress of hunger and homelessness that appears to be an inevitable outcome of such drastic and rapid changes? In Lech Walesa's words: "Nobody has previously taken the road that leads from socialism to capitalism."

Absolute suppression of religion has been a trademark of Marxism. Here, too, Gorbachev has taken the risk of change. It is quite clear that Marxism became religion. The Soviet people complacently accepted their oppression and let their leaders go unchallenged in the temples of power. But then the "pope" cried heresy and included himself under the label. Gorbachev now has supported the re-emergence of religion, and he has slowly loosened the restraints on the church. The State Council of Church Affairs, which essentially controls religious life, has lifted the ban on charitable work by the church. The Communist Party allowed a year-long millennial celebration of the church in Russia, lifted postal restrictions on religious materials (including Bibles) being shipped into the Soviet Union, has returned more than one thousand church buildings to the people, and has authorized more than 1,600 new religious associations. The World Council of Churches held its international gathering in Moscow in 1989, and the Lausanne Committee for World Evangelization hosted a nationwide conference with more than 300 Soviet Christian leaders, plotting means to evangelize the entire nation.

The risk taken by Gorbachev in leading this revolution only underlines his stature. To fail the people could bring a horrendous backlash from his coleaders, who would take the discontent as a mandate to return to Marxism with ever greater passion and control; Gorbachev would be publicly disgraced for betraying his own people and the great thrust of history toward the Marxist ideal. But Peter Drucker, management guru of the West, predicts that "within 25 years, if not sooner, the Russian empire will have disappeared. In fact, the more Gorbachev's perestroika succeeds in reviving a decaying Russian economy, the faster will the Russian empire unravel."[10] In other words, if Gorbachev improves his people's lives, he loses his empire. Perhaps his predecessors realized the cost of true success and were simply unwilling to pay the price.

The greatest internal risk faced by Gorbachev is ethnic unrest. The Soviet Union consists of 50 per cent Russians and 50 per cent ethnics (divided into fourteen major ethnic groups). *Glasnost* has lifted the lid on historical facts, which in these ethnics' cases read "cultural imperialism." The Soviet occupation of these ethnic regions is not unlike the colonial land-staking of Africa. Frustration, anger, resentment and bigotry have been bubbling under the surface, and a volcano is sure to erupt. Already the three Baltic states—Latvia, Estonia and Lithuania—have declared independence. Gorbachev has not recognized their new status and consequently is facing a public backlash from those who followed his lead toward independence. However, if Gorbachev recognizes the independence of one state, he faces losing fourteen states and half the Soviet population. The economics of these states and of Russia are so intertwined that no immediately simple solution seems to be available. In an unusual twist of geopolitics, George Bush, François Mitterand and Helmut Kohl have all asked the Baltics to delay their independence because of the conviction that it could hurt the greater good currently in progress.

At the international level, of course, Gorbachev has maneuvered a permanent moratorium on the expansionist ideals of Marxism. The threat is gone, and with it the ominous cold war overshadowing the decisions of politicians and the emotions of citizens for nearly half a century. Trillions of dollars and hundreds of millions of lives have been committed by the world's powers to that illusory tension, and it appears as if Gorbachev shut it down with the ease of a symphonic conductor—with a single wave of his hand through the air. The dilemma posed to both superpowers is that scores of industries and millions of jobs hang in the balance should the nations retreat from their Cold War postures.

Life after the Cold War

"Making war" has become our security, and now "making peace" is a greater threat for us than the posture of war. Our societies have become what we were fighting. Gorbachev's perception of the United States' vulnerability as a war society was poignantly described in his book, *Perestroika:*

> Those hoping to overstrain the Soviet Union seem too presumptuous about their own economic well-being. No matter how rich the USA is, it too can ill afford to throw away a third of a trillion dollars a year on armaments. The USA today borrows two thirds of what it spends on arms. The US federal debt is, in fact, the Pentagon's debt and will have to be repaid by many generations of Americans.[11]

A *Los Angeles Times* editorial asks, "What are we left with when Communism goes?" The writer wonders why so many Americans were left joyless by the great collapse. Our "market system" came out the victor, but we were left empty.

> Is this really what it's all about? Is the pursuit of self-interest the culmination of human political wisdom? Is such a smashing victory really coming to us—a bland, smug consumer society . . . ?[12]

The very ethical basis of our democratic capitalistic system will require a new scrutiny, and ethical people will be left with the conclusion that what makes us great is not *who we are not* (for example, communist) but rather *how we treat others.* An honest, humble review will suggest that repentance and change are in line.

Gorbachev has left us on the defensive, and ultimately that is for our good. In the past, our ethical frame of reference has been off. Perhaps the Soviet Union has been Satan's chief tool to keep the

Western church from taking serious ethical inventory of its own life. That roadblock has been removed and now a difficult way lies ahead for the United States. The postcommunist world has left us without a role in the world, which will be the focus of the next chapter.

Twenty years from now, tomorrow's youth will reflect on communism as today's youth reflect on Nazism. It will be a textbook story of what was. We live in that mystical moment of change that will never be recaptured. A vacuum exists that could easily be filled by similar "anti" postures—positions that lead more to presumption and self-righteousness than to moral, compassionate living. Our prayer should be for leaders and laypeople to seize the day for the true empire, the kingdom of God. As children of God, we will place our allegiances squarely in that camp and forge ahead with courage, justice, hope and humility.

God's kingdom never could fit into our pitiful categories of capitalist or democratic, but our pride of culture kept us blinded to this fact. God is about a new work today, and we have the opportunity to live as children of the day. Our righteous living could make the kingdoms of this world the kingdom of our God. That's what Jesus taught his disciples to pray for, and truly that is what the world is waiting for.

Thank God for Gorbachev's revolution. May we have the discernment to follow the Spirit in the days ahead as God leads us into the magnificent work of the kingdom, the only place where justice, dignity and righteousness truly will prevail.

8

The Fading Glory of the West

T HE decline of American power and prestige has been a slow, almost imperceptible crumbling. Consequently, few would say that the U.S. empire has fallen. But in a sense it has. Grand memories of our past and ethnocentric arrogance in the present keep us in a state of denial.

Did we think we could stand forever? Yes, we did. There's no evil in such a presumption, but there's no clear thinking in it either. The changing globe, the economic shifts, the emerging religious movements and powers, the skeletons in our political closets and the destructive consequences of our environmental and lifestyle choices are all affecting our present reality—a diminished "kingdom." For those of us whose only king is Jesus, earthly kingdoms carry only finite value. As the grass withers, so too kingdoms fade: God elevates a society for a short while and then raises up another.

But a shallow reading of history and a grossly misplaced sense of self-importance (perhaps connected errors) can delude us into thinking that we are God's channel of blessing to the world. Indeed, in President Reagan's words, "America's light is eternal, . . . every promise . . . still golden." Our shameless support of such nonsense indicates how grand is our delusion. The proliferation of preachers echoing this image underlines the desperate need for right thinking.

It would not be accurate to suggest that the United States was born a great empire and then declined. Many leaders have attempted a revision of our history that would make us a shining light from the outset. Our blatant disregard for the value of the lives and dignity of Native Americans never makes it into their talk about Manifest Destiny. Our near-genocide of these Americans, the importing of millions of Black slaves and close to a million Chinese slaves, and the inclusion of northern Mexico into our own territory are acts that reveal some of the less appealing principles on which this nation was founded.

The United States eventually became a great nation, or an empire, not in the moral sense but after the fashion of Great Britain. The indications of Britain's grandeur were a function of how far the empire reached, how many peoples it controlled, the size of its navy, the strength of its currency, the advancement of scientific knowledge and industry, and the number of kings who responded to its bidding. The United States became a great empire through massive territorial gains in the nineteenth century. Its military prowess developed a global reputation at the turn of the century as soldiers became the enforcers of governmental policies in Central America. Wealth flowed into the States as fruit and sugar industries took advantage of cheap labor and real estate in these same countries. The pinnacle of greatness was those few short years after our reluctant entrance into World War 2 and our defeat of the unquestionably evil empire of Adolf Hitler. The United States entered a heady era of dividing up the globe, dictating the redevelopment of Japan, sending thousands of missionaries abroad, and spending the pennies in a bottomless piggy bank. We became *the* leader of the democratic world and our own lifestyle was not questioned; the focus was on our "salvation" of others.

Just two decades later, we watched in horror as President John F. Kennedy and civil-rights leader Martin Luther King, Jr., were assassinated. Our kingdom was crumbling and we didn't know it.

The outside world watched as we sent soldiers on a routine military "clean-up job" in Southeast Asia. Yet our glory began to fade as we were forced to withdraw from Vietnam. The greatest military power in the world, the nation that blocked Hitler's international campaign, was defeated by a tiny population of brown-skinned people who were "backward" by Western standards. The most sophisticated equipment—B-52 bombers, *each* carrying payloads the size of World War 2's total explosives arsenal, and chemical weapons—and more than a million of the best-armed troops were no match for Vietnam's jungle soldiers. America went home humiliated. The Vietnam War lasted as long as it did precisely because of "image." If we could have won the war by staying in Vietnam, we would have. But military strategists came to understand that this was not a simple North-South battle over communism. Nationalistic pride was high throughout Vietnam, and U.S.-made weapons were regularly siphoned to North Vietnam by the South. (A significant number of U.S. casualties were inflicted by U.S. weapons.)

During the Vietnam War, Harris Morgenthau, consultant to the state and defense departments, described the U.S. dilemma in this way:

> The United States is not likely to win the war in the traditional way by breaking the enemy's will to resist, but rather by killing so many enemies that there is no one left to resist. Killing in war has traditionally been a means to a psychological end. In this war, killing becomes an end in itself. The physical elimination of the enemy and victory become synonyms. . . . *No civilized nation can wage such a war without suffering incalculable moral damage.*[1]

The United States has underestimated the impact Vietnam had on its empire. The failure was not in losing the war. It was much more profound. Morgenthau suggested that the United States withdraw ("liquidate the war," in his words), and he called for a specific action that has never been taken. "The United States should show that it is wise and strong enough to admit a mistake and correct it. The liquidation of misadventure need not affect its future policies."[2]

But U.S. involvement in Vietnam never has been resolved. The wounds of 55,000 families who lost children to that war still fester. Had victory in Vietnam been essential for the abatement of worldwide communism, America would have pressed the war with the same sort of determination that drove it to complete World War 2. The truth is, we had no business in Vietnam, and when it was clear that we were not facing a simple "clean-up job," we withdrew. The *failure* of Vietnam was our leaders' silence on the immorality of that war from the very beginning. We continue to suffer from this haughty spirit and lack of repentance. And this only doubles the pain of soldiers who now live with the fact that they trusted their leaders' call to duty and responded to the draft. Vietnam will remain a blight on the U.S. image abroad—both as a military defeat and as a moral failure.

Subsequent foreign adventurisms in the name of justice and democracy have either failed or stirred up a chorus of anti-American slogans. We failed to overthrow Castro in Cuba; our "successful" invasion of Grenada was condemned by Latin American leaders, as was our invasion of Panama. When the Central American presidents unanimously called for the dismantling of the *contras,* our president responded by increasing the *contras'* funding.

Korean students are burning the American flag over the U.S.-supported government's killing of several hundred students in the 1980 Kwangju demonstration (41,000 U.S. troops are stationed in South Korea); peasants in Guatemala and El Salvador have suffered more than 100,000 deaths with the help of U.S. tax dollars that support right-wing governments and their military arms. Muslims have turned against the States over the CIA coup in Iran and the support of Nusi Said of Iraq, Hussein I of Jordan, Hassan II of Morocco and Anwar Sadat of Egypt. South African Blacks consider the United States pro-apartheid; Pakistanis still resent the United States' earlier support of Zia al-Haq.

The United States took its victory in World War 2 as a mandate to police the world, and each step in that direction seems to have damaged its image. In many parts of the world, economic and social ills are uncritically attributed to CIA involvement. Whether or not the CIA contributed to these *specific* incidents and problems is not the issue. What is important is the American reputation for interfering in the affairs of other sovereign nations.

Thomas Perry Thornton, editor of the *Annals of the American Academy of Political and Social Science,* offers this analysis:

> Precisely because the United States was everywhere, it saw itself as the custodian of global interests that transcended the parochial concerns of nations with lesser responsibilities. The

United States often acted with sovereign disregard for others' interests, and the victims of our attentions responded with a vehemence that reflected the urgency of their concern. The belligerence, even violence, that had been directed against the colonial powers in India or West Africa before World War II now began to be turned against the United States, for we had become the frontline guardians of an international order that was inevitably felt as oppressive by many. We often behaved with an incredible intrusiveness that was irritating even when well meant.[3]

Mexican intellectual Carlos Fuentes says that the United States is a sort of Jekyll-and-Hyde government: democracy on the inside, but empire in its behavior toward the outside. The Soviet Union, Fuentes says, is at least consistent in that it is an empire both within and without. The United States' incoherence makes it profoundly hypocritical from a Third World point of view.[4]

These harsh images from abroad were easily brushed aside because of the presence of expansionistic Marxism. Perhaps it is kinder to say that the presence of Marxism blinded us to our own abuses abroad, but it's fair to assume that grown men and women in leadership were using the existence of Marxism to their advantage in pursuing certain international goals. Gorbachev's revolution has put our own history smack in front of us now; unusual leadership will be required if we are to honestly inventory this heritage. Christians who are brave enough to rise to this challenge against the popular tide of culture will be the truly great leaders in America's tomorrow.

A Fading Glory
Several other items have contributed to the fading U.S. glory. Islamic students were able to hold fifty-two Americans hostage for

444 days, and even then the hostages were released because of negotiations—our sophisticated Delta force failed to rescue them.

Then there are hijackings, the blowing up of TWA and Pan Am jets, the murder of 241 U.S. Marines in Lebanon, America's status as a debtor nation (with the largest foreign debt in the world), the power held over us by indebted Third World governments that owe our banks so much money they may never pay back the principal, the OPEC oil embargo, and our inability to contain terrorist incidents directed against our citizens.

In addition to this vulnerability, certain Third World and Islamic leaders are decrying the U.S. presence in their countries because, they claim, we bring moral decline to their societies: pornography, drunkenness and sexual promiscuity. And wherever U.S. military bases are found, prostitution abounds, sexually transmitted diseases spread and fatherless children are reared in the gutters.

Leaving the world behind and returning to the security of our own nation, we're confronted with the state of our inner kingdom. Foreign capital is now buying out the States much as we were buying into foreign countries decades ago. More than 25 per cent of Los Angeles' downtown real estate is owned by Japanese corporations, as is the historic Rockefeller Center in New York City, a great center of art and journalism that houses NBC studios and the Associated Press. When last did we buy an American-made TV, VCR or compact disc player? Americans say they prefer Japanese-built cars because they're more reliable and sensitive to the driver's needs.

Since 1982 the United States has been running a trade deficit with the rest of the world, and consequently more than $660 billion in foreign money has made capital gain in the past seven years.[5] The States used to possess 40 per cent of the world's wealth; that proportion has declined to 20 per cent. The interest that accumulates on U.S. debt is $8,000 *per second.* Our government has borrowed more than $300 billion from foreign countries to service this debt.[6]

A Moral Lapse

We have lost our very own soul. We are a nation of people fraught with tremendous human need and immorality, and we callously step over each other's bodies.

We have listened as a recent president denied any significant physical need in the land and suggested that our homeless citizens were homeless only because they preferred living outdoors. Polls consistently show that the public believes its leaders lie. Ivan Boesky, fined $100 million for defrauding the public, told students at the University of California at Berkeley's commencement, "Greed is all right, by the way; I want you to know that. I think greed is healthy." This is a moral lapse, not a mere "memory lapse," and it will have long-term ramifications.

Pete Rose, the all-American baseball hero, turned out to be a convicted criminal. The governmental agency for Housing and Urban Development became a jackpot for the rich. Each year almost 600,000 teens attempt suicide—5,000 of those succeed. Seven Americans were killed onboard the space shuttle *Challenger* because of the tragic carelessness of scientists fighting deadlines and managers pushing the profit margin. And not too far behind us are student shootings at Kent State, assassinations in Dallas, Memphis and Los Angeles, and the scandal of Watergate.

Our children are becoming the "indentured youth" of tomorrow because Congress has given its primary attention to winning elections. We have "put our children's future on the auction block, insisting on putting money into the hands of the wealthy and weapons into the arsenals of generals—instead of research funds into our civilian economy and food into the lunch boxes of our kids."[7] In education, 75 per cent of high-school students are unable to write a letter seeking employment; more than 50 per cent of the nation's twenty-year-olds are unable to add up their lunch bills. Compared to other students around the world, U.S. students ranked fourteenth in ninth-grade science (tied with Thailand and Singapore).[8] The United States faces a shortage of more than 500,000 trained chemists, biologists, physicists and engineers due to poor training. Economically, the nation will not be able to compete with emerging economic powers in the near future.

Violence is a desperate problem in the United States. Every day seventy-four people die from wounds inflicted by handguns. That's 30,000 per year—more than half the number of U.S. soldiers killed in the Vietnam War. The FBI reports that between 1983 and 1987, arrests of those *under eighteen* for murder increased 22.2 per cent; for aggravated assault, 18.6 per cent; and for rape, 14.6 per cent. And that against a teen-population *decline* of 2 per cent.[9] Reported child abuse cases in 1987: 2.2 million. By age sixteen, a child will typically have seen 200,000 acts of violence on TV, including 33,000 murders. A new verb has been added to American dictionaries: "wilding," the practice of a sport in which youth walk the streets in search of opportunity to rape, mug, steal and murder—just for the fun of it.

A glance at additional statistics tells again of the decline of the empire: twenty per cent of all youth live under the poverty line; 32 million of all Americans live below that line. Four million are homeless (and at least 220,000 of them are school-aged children), and 325,000 foster kids are shuttled among the 125,000 foster homes. In 1989, substance-abusing mothers gave birth to 375,000 babies; 470,000 were born to single, unemployed teen-age mothers. Twenty-five per cent of all pregnant women receive no prenatal care, while the United States ranks eighteenth internationally in infant mortality. Four million Americans are addicted to cocaine, 700,000 Americans are in prison, and twenty-five per cent of high-school students drop out before receiving their diploma.[10] One out of two marriages ends in divorce, one million teen-agers get pregnant each year, one million teen-agers run away from home each year and 1.5 million babies are aborted each year.

From Empire to Kingdom

For those of us who choose to live in the reality of our faded empire and make a difference for Christ's kingdom within that context, at least four responses are necessary. First, we need to take a frank moral inventory of our heritage and current circumstances and take action in light of the discoveries we make. At the top of this inventory is the treatment of indigenous Americans, imported slaves, and our imperialistic, greedy posture toward the rest of the world. The church does not have the right to stand in the public square and demand fair treatment of babies-in-the-womb if it has yet to be heard in that same town square confessing the sins of racism, arrogance and callousness to the poor. We will know that we have begun to head down this road when the more prominent evangelical leaders of our day identify themselves with this history. If the church is not convinced of its need to settle moral accounts, it will have no power to engage society in the current moral issues. We will be labeled rightly as hypocrites and fakes.

Second, we must keep the focus of responsibility on ourselves and not society. The temptation is there, when facing the evils of our day, to blame "secular humanists," "liberals" or "the press." The truth is, if the United States is 99 per cent evangelized, as mission statistician David Barrett suggests, then the church is to blame for the mess we are in. Is this where our evangelism leads? Is this what a society looks like after the gospel has been unleashed without restraint for 300 years? The plight of society is nothing more than an indictment on the church. Hatred for the evils of our society should be channeled into resolve to truly live as children of light, under the rule of God's love and righteousness. We should be profoundly disturbed that our fruit is hard to find, and we should be greatly motivated to become the very aroma of Christ to broken, wicked people.

Third, we need to link together in the cause of justice. Christians from both the liberal and conservative ends of the continuum have recognized the need to confront evil structures. On the one end, we have tended to attack the systems of racism and economics that keep people prisoners. On the other end, we have fought the structural evils that allow 1.5 million babies to be aborted annually. We have recognized how, in this context, justice must prevail: Systemic oppression of the unborn must be overcome. Because both sides have fought structural injustices, now they can come together in the battle that will represent one congregation of people whose biblical agenda makes them ready to embrace all of society with the good news of Christ. A deep integrity will emerge in the church that will silence the mouths of naysayers who are used to hearing spiritualized language that has little impact on society's ills.

Finally, we must renounce the temptation of power. God gives influence to those who serve his purposes in time. The biblical Esther was one such person. She had influence at the highest level of power, yet she had to risk her position and her life by approaching the king with a moral request concerning the Jewish people. I don't believe we understand the words of Jesus, who said that we are being sent out as sheep among wolves. When Christ stood silent before Herod, all the heavens knew that the existence of the entire Roman court was at stake at that moment. Jesus could have brought fire down from heaven, but instead he went to the cross. He gave us the command to go in the same manner he did: "As the Father sent me, so send I you."

Christians must be unimpressed with power. Yes, we pray for the kingdoms of this world, and we hope that our influence on them will draw their little empires closer to *the* kingdom. But we know that ultimately Caesar is no friend to Jesus, and we serve only Jesus.

The empire of the West has fallen. But our redeemed sense of what matters takes us beyond that fact. We have come to understand that while earthly kingdoms come and go, Jesus will reign forever. It is to the enterprise of his kingdom that we give ourselves, fully and joyfully, knowing that we are led from victory to victory and eventually into the very courtyard of the great and awesome King. May God grant us the grace to walk every day in the service of this King and to say no to the power and kingdoms of this world. May we have the discernment of Jesus, who, when tempted by Satan to take power over all the earth, called Satan's power what it truly was—temptation—and instead went the way of the cross.

9

The Evangelism Crisis

HOWEVER one reads the statistics, the world is desperately unsaved.

In A.D. 100, the global population was 181.5 million—180.5 million non-Christians and one million Christians. By the year 2000, the global population will be 6.3 billion—4.3 billion non-Christians and 2 billion Christians. The "bright" side of the picture, as some have tried to paint it, is that in A.D. 100 the world was only 0.6 per cent Christian, versus the 32.3 per cent predicted for the year 2000. However, from 1985 to 2000, the total number of non-Christians will increase by one billion people to a total of 4.3 billion. The global Christian population has declined over the last 100 years from 34.4 per cent to 32.3 per cent.[1]

Fundamental to evangelicalism is the conviction that there is no saving access to God aside from a personal relationship with Jesus Christ. In this world and in the world to come, life outside of Christ is hell. At the current growth rate of the non-Christian population, each day hell grows by 187,000 people.[2]

For those of us who love Jesus, this represents nothing less than a crisis. Our new life has given us a compassion that longs for everyone to know Jesus' love. Like him, we have a deep desire that no one should perish and that everyone, while on earth, should enjoy the forgiveness of sins and the abundant life of Christ.

The Unevangelized Belt

In trying to present us with a means of understanding the demands of world evangelism, researchers David Barrett and Patrick Johnstone have divided up the globe according to several different grids. Their most common measurement—the evangelized versus the unevangelized—is a qualitative measure of how much a specific country has been *exposed* to the gospel, indicating whether or not people there have been presented with a good opportunity to receive Christ. Of the 251 nations of the world, Barrett's statistics show 183 nations more than 90 per cent evangelized, sixty-three nations between 20 to 90 per cent evangelized, and only five nations less than 20 per cent evangelized.[3]

Barrett's research offers a contrasting view of those same nations based on *response* to the gospel (measured by affiliated church membership) versus *exposure*. On the response scale, Barrett lists fifty-two nations with a church membership greater than 90 per cent, one-hundred forty-five nations with membership between 20 to 90 per cent, and sixty-four nations with membership less than 20 per cent.

The words that most aptly describe these least-churched people are Asian, urban and Islamic. Just as in the United States, where we have the so-called Bible Belt of the South, so, stretching from the Mediterranean Sea through central and south Asia to China, is the *Unevangelized Belt.* This belt includes the Islamic peoples of northern Africa, the Middle East, Iran, Afghanistan, Soviet Central Asia, Pakistan, India and Indonesia; and the Hindu and Buddhist peoples of India, Japan and China.

On the rim of the Mediterranean, where Christianity was born and first propagated, the fifteen cities with populations greater than one million are now totally Islamic. Other great Asian cities such as Bangkok, Calcutta, Delhi, Tokyo, Beijing, Dacca and Jakarta have only a minute Christian presence.

As Islam and nationalism sweep these territories, Christianity has suffered from the stigma of association with the West.

Isolated from the Gospel

Mission researchers have also attempted to describe the challenge of world evangelism according to groups of people that apparently live isolated from a gospel witness. Ed Dayton, founder of Mission Advanced Research and Communication Center (MARC), first introduced this helpful concept to the Lausanne Congress on World Evangelization in 1974, as a strategic method of carrying out the Great Commission. The person most responsible for popularizing Dayton's strategy is Ralph Winter, founder of the U.S. Center for World Mission. Winter introduced the term "hidden people" to designate these groups of people, later substituting the term "unreached peoples."

Originally, Winter printed charts and graphs alleging the existence of 17,000 unreached-peoples groups. Yet the count seemed rather informal and uncertain—later it was revised to 12,000 unreached-peoples groups.

David Barrett has picked up the task of measuring the existence of unreached peoples in a more precise fashion. His research shows a total of 432 "macropeoples" in the world. These are identified primarily along racial lines. The actual number of ethnolinguistic people groups in the world (subsets of the 432) comes to approximately 11,500. According to Barrett, close to 2,000 of these groups have little significant Christian presence—that is, they are the unreached peoples. Barrett says they add up to approximately 1.3 billion people. He has produced a list of the largest 150 unreached-peoples groups, which make up one billion of the 1.3 billion unreached, showing the extent to which they have been *exposed* to the gospel. (All but four groups, he says, are more than 10 per cent evangelized in this sense.)

The *response* to the gospel in these groups constitutes the real evangelistic challenge, according to Barrett. The majority of them are less than 5 per cent affiliated with a church.[4] It is interesting that almost all of these groups lie within the Unevangelized Belt.

Meeting the Missions Challenge

There are several ways to respond to this evangelistic challenge. The simplest and least honest approach is to ignore the crisis of lostness, dodging behind fancy theological formulations. The sovereignty of God is a fact, and his final responsibility for both the temporal and the eternal plight of humankind is unquestionable.

But only an unloving person can shut out the unsaved world simply because God is sovereign. Scripture offers us a pristinely clear picture of the deep love of this sovereign God and how that led to the painful, sacrificial death at Calvary. Christ tells us that we are to go into the world as the Father sent him. It is not an academic theological issue, it is a question that belongs to our identity—that is, Christ *in us,* the hope of glory, the incarnation of the word of life in today's society. We live tension. On the one hand, there are so many unsaved people, there has been so little progress in the evangelistic task. But on the other hand, a miracle occurs each time someone passes from death to new life in Christ.

Approximately 40,000 U.S. Christians now live overseas as career missionaries with the express purpose of communicating Christ across cultures. That does not represent an overwhelming response to this evangelistic crisis; it equals one missionary for every ten churches in the States and a fraction of the million-plus full-time Christian workers here.

Although the U.S. church bears only part of the responsibility for world missions, it is helpful to measure the ratio of North American missionaries to the number of people in the Unevangelized Belt: one to 32,500. Actually, the total number of North American missionaries working in the Belt itself is 5,229, or 13 per cent of the current missionary task force. That percentage would be much smaller were it not for the fact that Japan and Indonesia are in the Belt; these two countries receive more than half of the missionaries to this area of need (2,931 missionaries total).[5]

The North American Protestant missionary enterprise obviously has room to expand. There are a total of 395 mission agencies that send career missionaries overseas, and a mere fifteen of these organizations account for half of all the missionaries. Six agencies—the Southern Baptists, Youth With A Mission, Wycliffe Bible Translators, New Tribes Mission, Christian Churches and Assemblies of God—account for more than 34 per cent of all U.S. missionaries. One-third of all U.S. missionaries work in only eight of the world's 251 nations: Brazil, the Philippines, Japan, Mexico, Kenya, Indonesia, Papua New Guinea and Zaire.[6]

Overcoming the Barriers to Missions

Quite obviously, relocating a family overseas for missions is no small matter. Responding to the stresses related to that job requires a deep spirituality and a sure sense of calling. The cost of separation from family, friends and the familiar is higher than most of us are trained to bear. Yet we must pray that God will grant the North American church the sort of maturity that will prepare its members for crosscultural mission. The luxury of our comfortable Western lifestyle has unfortunately insulated us from the experiences of scarcity, hardship and suffering that reflect Christ's call in Philippians 2 to leave our places of privilege and power in order to serve others.

Another barrier to crosscultural missions is the financial cost. Unfortunately, this too clearly reflects a cultural influence on missions. Families are expected to raise exorbitant amounts of money, often in excess of $40,000 per year, to serve in Third World countries. Not only are many "would-bes" prevented from going because they fail to raise their support, but many who do go are prevented from effective ministry because their lifestyles far exceed those of the nationals they serve. They are thus isolated from the possibility of true friendship and equality.

It is going to take a new sort of missionary to meet this evangelistic challenge. It will require people who can live simply and humbly, in difficult circumstances and vulnerable to nationals.

The evangelistic challenge will require new mission structures. The mission agency of the coming decade will be one that serves as a broker to partner Western Christians with national Christians. Standard of living and job descriptions will be determined by, and oversight provided by, Christian leaders in the Unevangelized Belt. Mission structures will discover that they can deploy a much higher number of missionaries (because of the lower costs involved) and spend less on financial overhead due to less responsibility for management in the foreign culture.

A final challenge of the Unevangelized Belt is the missionary visa. Ninety per cent of those countries are called "closed" or "limited access" in that they do not issue missionary visas. All of these countries, however, permit foreigners to enter as either business employees or students. Even Mongolia, the most restrictive of all, has now put out invitations for Western industry. Currently more than 400,000 Americans are employed overseas—a group ten times the size of the missionary task force. Finding employment in the Unevangelized Belt won't require too much creativity of Western Christians who earnestly seek a role of ministry there.

One last word regarding the evangelism crisis: Some evangelicals in the West have attempted to polarize the ministries of evangelism and social responsibility. They have argued that we cannot afford to focus our energies on both and that in fact the one (social responsibility) is not so much a biblical requirement as an option. Christians who propagate that view are not biblically literate. God has quite simply called the church to bring *all elements* of his kingdom to bear on the earth. It borders on blasphemy to suggest that the sovereign God cannot provide the church with all it requires to faithfully engage the wholistic ministry of the kingdom, and it certainly *is* blasphemy to suggest that justice and compassion are optional attributes of God. They are central to his identity and as such are central to the identity of people who go out as his ambassadors.

Third World leaders often suffer under the legacy of missionaries who considered elements of our calling optional. The gospel witness lacks integrity in many suffering parts of the world where the missionary has sided with the oppressor in the name of "neutrality" or "evangelism-only." South Africa is an example. Black leaders regularly refer to missionaries as people who gave them the Bible and stole their land.

The Lord has been raising up a new generation of young evangelicals who accept all the commands of the Lord: They feed the hungry, they work for justice, and they preach the forgiveness of sins. They will find a warm welcome in the Unevangelized Belt.

10

The Internationalization of the Gospel

S PANISH is the language most spoken by Christians around the world; English is second. In 1800, 86 per cent of all Christians were White; by the year 2000 that proportion will have dropped to 39 per cent. The world's largest congregation is in Korea, the biggest church building in Côte d'Ivoire (formerly Ivory Coast).

From a purely statistical point of view, Christianity is a non-Western religion. This reality has yet to impact the majority of us in the United States, but we will experience it in the final decade of the twentieth century.

The power and influence of Christianity's new leadership will be felt in a variety of ways: the top theological schools will be in Asia and Latin America; new questions on theology and praxis will

emerge reflecting the social, economic and political realities of
Third World living; few Whites will occupy plenary posts at Christian
conventions; presidents of denominations will have last names we
cannot pronounce (as will authors of forthcoming best-selling Christian books); a European-based reading of church history will take
a back seat to other traditions of world Christianity; and TV evangelists of all colors will be preaching to us in our living rooms. The
shift of the "power base" to the Third World is not exclusive to
Christianity. As the stature and glory of the West have been fading,
the stature and sense of self of the Third World have been growing.

Christian leaders from the West are often stunned by the harsh
words of Third World Christian leaders who reflect on the North
American church. Were we as Westerners more attuned to the
issues of the Third World, we would quickly understand the need
for humility and listening. We would see how our history of global
expansion has brought with it slavery, economic injustice, political
domination, war, apartheid and the like. The church of the West
has been too slow to denounce its complicitous role in the evils
of the past. Emerging Christian leaders of the Third World distin-
guish between Christ and cultural/economic imperialism, and
they refuse to cooperate with the latter. As the world cries out for
justice and dignity, so do these Christian leaders—who are the
future leaders of the worldwide church.

In the pages that follow, I suggest that there are several significant adjustments the Western church will need to make if it hopes
to contribute to the future of global Christianity. Change is a natural and necessary part of growing. The world has changed and
so must we—anchored to the Rock, but geared to the times.

Dancing to a New Band

We need to make it our pattern to defer to non-Western opinions and ideas whenever our most basic convictions are not at stake. Western wealth and isolation have kept us from understanding the real issues of the Third World, yet we continue to impose our agenda there. Few international Christian conferences are truly international: the programs, invitation lists and venues are usually controlled by Westerners, even though the events happen "over there."

Donors in the West have undue power over the missionaries they send. Policies governing missionaries' lives are often a function of decisions made in Wheaton, Atlanta, Colorado Springs or Pasadena because "donors must not be offended." Policies should be made by nationals who better understand their cultural histories, politics and economics.

There is no country in the world where God has not raised up mature, adequate national leadership to guide the activities of foreign guests. Yet I continue to meet Western mission leaders overseas who assert that even though they have worked in one location for over fifty years, they are unable to find non-Western leaders capable of guiding their ministry. Only arrogance and racism cripple the search for national leaders.

Presidents and professors of America's theological institutions need to acquaint themselves with the views of non-Western theologians, whose texts need to become staples in Western seminaries. Even the theological schools of mission are not making this obvious adjustment. In the last year five major vacancies at the top three mission schools in the United States were filled by White Western men. If the *administrators* are not choosing to change these patterns, a very painful road toward true partnership is ahead. Jesus, a non-White baby born to refugee parents fleeing to Egypt, became the Messiah of the world. All of his disciples were non-White, and to them he entrusted the Great Commission. We are their spiritual offspring.

Adjusting to this internationalization of the gospel is a very difficult process. Several Christian leaders who have attempted it have suffered from decreased donations and rumors of their "going liberal." These unfair responses are perhaps part of the price of change. It is time for an unusually brave leadership to emerge to get us through this transition; it is time for new *organizations* to emerge whose very operations will be built on these new realities at the outset.

Embracing Social Justice

Social justice is central to the Third World Christian's understanding of the nature and work of God. Extreme forms of liberation theology are the consequence in part of Western church leaders' refusal to allow the justice of God to be taught and practiced in the crosscultural mission of the church. Evangelical institutions need to engage in serious theological work that puts justice and evangelism together—as partners rather than enemies. Seminaries that allow students to graduate without wrestling with these issues are simply irresponsible.

An encouraging sign in this area is the level of interest at the student level in the United States. I continually encounter young adults who easily accept that Christians provide homes for the homeless and food for the hungry, extend Jesus' forgiveness to the lost and work for justice. I believe this is the future student movement in the United States. We can be grateful for this indication that God has gone ahead to prepare future crosscultural servants from the States who will have strong partnership relations with the Third World church.

We must emphatically assert that the "new liberals" of the twenty-first century will be those who choose to exclude *either* the salvation of Jesus *or* the justice of Jesus from our Christian identity. Both these groups of people will be selling individuals and societies short of the good news of God's kingdom and will be teaching by example that only parts of Scripture are relevant to following God in today's world.

Christians who honestly and clearly articulate the wholistic call of the Scriptures to our current evangelical youth will be the leaders of tomorrow's church.

Building Bridges in the Church

New faces, strange names, different theological concepts, a rainbow of colors. David Barrett's *World Christian Encyclopedia* lists over 22,000 denominations worldwide. This is our family, and yet we don't seem to get along very well. Obviously, we Christians have strong opinions about the way our faith should be lived out.

The internationalization of the gospel will increase our exposure to people who call themselves *Christian,* but whose ideas and behavior are different enough from ours to cause us to withdraw rather than pursue fellowship.

The most serious implication of this reaction is that we often end up labeling people unlike ourselves as dangerous, cultic, liberal or aberrational—when, really, they're just different. (Although I don't wish to deny the existence of groups that are indeed dangerous.) The recent international gathering of 5,000 evangelical mission leaders in Manila had subgroups that would not fellowship with each other. The magazine I formerly edited, *World Christian,* asked a particular mission agency for slides that depicted a tribe of people totally unreached with the gospel of Jesus Christ. That agency declined, explaining that some of the magazine's readers are charismatic and the agency's leaders didn't want charismatics to go as missionaries to those people.

What brings us all together is the deep love of Jesus, who has given us new life. Our lives have become an offering of thanks to Jesus, best expressed in our lifestyles of compassion toward "the least of these" in our world. Our guide is Scripture inspired by the Spirit. Specific labels are not as important in the days ahead as we begin to fellowship with the international family. Evangelical, Roman Catholic, fundamentalist, charismatic, ecumenical, Pentecostal—all these terms carry historical baggage but do not adequately describe the people to whom they are applied. We should assume a humble posture of listening to and learning from each other. All of us bring strengths and deficiencies to the fellowship hall and *need* the perspective of each other.

Fear is a strong force in keeping us apart. A love for Jesus and a desire to understand more of his truth can counter that fear and help launch us on an exciting journey of meeting others who have been saved by Calvary love. We'll be surprised to discover how many brothers and sisters we have in Christ.

Thinking Globally, Acting Locally

Most of us have impact on the world's events through our prayer lives, fewer of us perhaps by our donations to global enterprises. Our individual responses to environmental issues impact a little of the world, as do our lobbying efforts through groups such as Bread for the World. Some of us have direct and much more meaningful impact by relocating crossculturally. None of us has to live an irrelevant life.

The major cities of the United States are beginning to look as if the world has moved to our very doorstep. Theologies of church growth and strategies of evangelism that are dreamed up in the boardrooms of suburban churches will be irrelevant in such environments. In addition, poverty, homelessness, drug abuse and violence have become as American as apple pie; churches need to relocate to places of such urban hardship. Watch for the church leaders who are brave enough to move their congregations into these areas: they will discover a much richer Bible as they return to it for insights into their ministry, and they will find themselves much closer to Third World Christians. If these churches send out crosscultural missionaries, they will have discipled servants who have less of a lifestyle and theological gap to bridge when teaming up with Christians in the Third World.

In the same way, the mission agencies providing significant leadership to tomorrow's generation of crosscultural servants will be those that grapple with their insulation from the real issues concerning their Third World partners. Some courageous decisions will be made to move headquarters into ghettos and other places of poverty.

All of us have the option and privilege of locally living out the global implications of our faith. That, ultimately, is what a "world Christian" is. We can take leadership in our own situations. We can join with friends. We can forge relevant lives in tomorrow's global society.

Appendix

The Oxford Declaration on Christian Faith and Economics and the Lausanne Covenant are important documents that offer an evangelical and globally oriented basis for Christian thought and action in the next decade and beyond. I include them here as worthy foundations for our missions strategy.

The Oxford Declaration on Christian Faith and Economics

Preamble

The Oxford Declaration on Christian Faith and Economics of January, 1990, is issued jointly by over 100 theologians and economists, ethicists and development practitioners, church leaders and business managers who come from various parts of the world. We live in diverse cultures and subcultures, are steeped in differing traditions of theological and economic thinking, and therefore have diverse notions as to how Christian faith and economic realities should intersect. We have found this diversity enriching even when we could not reach agreement. At the same time we rejoice over the extent of unanimity on the complex economics of today made possible by our common profession of faith in our Lord Jesus Christ.

We affirm that through his life, death, resurrection, and ascension to glory, Christ has made us one people (Gal. 3:28). Though living in different cultures, we acknowledge together that there is one body and one Spirit, just as we are called to the one hope, one Lord, one faith, one baptism, and one God and Father of us all (Eph. 4:4).

We acknowledge that a Christian search for truth is both a communal and an individual effort. As part of the one people in Christ, each of us wants to comprehend the relevance of Christ to the great issues facing humanity today together "with all the saints" (Eph. 3:18). All our individual insights need to be corrected by the perspectives of the global Christian community as well as Christians through the centuries.

We affirm that Scripture, the word of the living and true God, is our supreme authority in all matters of faith and conduct. Hence we turn to Scripture as our reliable guide in reflection on issues concerning economic, social, and political life. As economists and theologians we desire to submit both theory and practice to the bar of Scripture.

Together we profess that God, the sovereign of life, in love made a perfect world for human beings created to live in fellowship with God. Although our greatest duty is to honor and glorify God, we rebelled against God, fell from our previous harmonious relationship with God, and brought evil upon ourselves and God's world. But God did not give up on the creation. As Creator, God continues patiently working to overcome the evil which was perverting the creation. The central act of God's redemptive new creation is the death, resurrection and reign in glory of Jesus Christ, the Son of God, and the sending of the Holy Spirit. This restoration will only be completed at the end of human history and the reconciliation of all things.

Justice is basic to Christian perspectives on economic life. Justice is rooted in the character of God. "For the Lord is righteous, he loves justice" (Ps. 11:7). Justice expresses God's actions to restore God's provision to those who have been deprived and to punish those who have violated God's standards.

A. Creation and Stewardship

God the Creator

1. From God and through God and to God are all things (Rom. 11:36). In the freedom of God's eternal love, by the word of God's omnipotent power, and through the Creator Spirit, the Triune God gave being to the world and to human beings who live in it. God pronounced the whole creation good. For its continuing existence creation is dependent on God. The same God who created it is present in it, sustaining it and giving it bountiful life (Ps. 104:29). In Christ, "all things were created . . . and all things hold together" (Col. 1:15-20). Though creation owes its being to God, it is itself not divine. The greatness of creation—both human and nonhuman—exists to glorify its Creator. The divine origin of the creation, its continued existence through God, redemption through Christ, and its purpose to glorify God are fundamental truths which must guide all Christian reflection on creation and stewardship.

Stewardship of Creation

2. God the Creator and Redeemer is the ultimate owner. "The earth is the Lord's and the fullness thereof" (Ps. 24:1). But God has entrusted the earth to human beings to be responsible for it on God's behalf. They should work as God's stewards in the creative,

faithful management of the world, recognizing that they are responsible to God for all they do with the world and to the world.

3. God created the world and pronounced it "very good" (Gen. 1:31). Because of the fall and the resulting curse, creation "groans in travail" (Rom. 8:22). The thoughtlessness, greed, and violence of sinful human beings have damaged God's good creation and produced a variety of ecological problems and conflicts. When we abuse and pollute creation, as we are doing in many instances, we are poor stewards and invite disaster in both local and global ecosystems.

4. Much of human aggression toward creation stems from a false understanding of the nature of creation and the human role in it. Humanity has constantly been confronted by the two challenges of selfish individualism, which neglects human community, and rigid collectivism, which stifles human freedom. Christians and others have often pointed out both dangers. But only recently have we realized that both ideologies have a view of the world with humanity at the center which reduces material creation to a mere instrument.

5. Biblical life and world view are not centered on humanity. They are God-centered. Nonhuman creation was not made exclusively for human beings. We are repeatedly told in the Scripture that all things—human beings and the environment in which they live—were "for God" (Rom. 11:36; 1 Cor. 8:6; Col. 1:16). Correspondingly, nature is not merely the raw material for human activity. Though only human beings have been made in the image of God, nonhuman creation too has a dignity of its own, so much so that after the flood God established a covenant not only with Noah and his descendants, but also "with every living creature that is with you" (Gen. 9:9). Similarly, the Christian hope for the future also includes creation. "The creation itself will be set free from its bond-

age to decay and obtain the glorious liberty of the children of God" (Rom. 8:21).

6. The dominion which God gave human beings over creation (Gen. 1:30) does not give them license to abuse creation. First, they are responsible to God, in whose image they were made, not to ravish creation but to sustain it, as God sustains it in divine providential care. Second, since human beings are created in the image of God for community and not simply as isolated individuals (Gen. 1:28), they are to exercise dominion in a way that is responsible to the needs of the total human family, including future generations.

7. Human beings are both part of creation and also unique. Only human beings are created in the image of God. God thus grants human beings dominion over the nonhuman creation (Gen. 1:28–30). But dominion is not domination. According to Genesis 2:15, human dominion over creation consists in the twofold task of "tilling and taking care" of the garden. Therefore all work must have not only a productive but also a protective aspect. Economic systems must be shaped so that a healthy ecological system is maintained over time. All responsible human work done by the stewards of God the Sustainer must contain an element of cooperation with the environment.

Stewardship and Economic Production

8. Economic production results from the stewardship of the earth which God assigned to humanity. While materialism, injustice, and greed are in fundamental conflict with the teaching of the whole Scripture, there is nothing in Christian faith that suggests that the production of new goods and services is undesirable. Indeed, we are explicitly told that God "richly furnishes us with everything to enjoy" (1 Tim. 6:17). Production is not only necessary

to sustain life and make it enjoyable; it also provides an opportunity for human beings to express their creativity in the service of others. In assessing economic systems from a Christian perspective, we must consider their ability both to generate and to distribute wealth and income justly.

Technology and Its Limitations

9. Technology mirrors the basic paradox of the sinfulness and goodness of human nature. Many current ecological problems result from the extensive use of technology after the onset of industrialization. Though technology has liberated human beings from some debasing forms of work, it has also often dehumanized other forms of work. Powerful nations and corporations that control modern technology are regularly tempted to use it to dominate the weak for their own narrow self-interest. As we vigorously criticize the negative effects of technology, we should, however, not forget its positive effects. Human creativity is expressed in the designing of tools for celebration and work. Technology helps us meet the basic needs of the world population and to do so in ways which develop the creative potential of individuals and societies. Technology can also help us reverse environmental devastation. A radical rejection of modern technology is unrealistic. Instead we must search for ways to use appropriate technology responsibly according to every cultural context.

10. What is technologically possible is not necessarily morally permissible. We must not allow technological development to follow its own inner logic, but must direct it to serve moral ends. We acknowledge our limits in foreseeing the impact of technological change and encourage an attitude of humility with respect to technological innovation. Therefore, continuing evaluation of the impact of technological change is essential. Four criteria derived

from Christian faith help us to evaluate the development and use of technology. First, technology should not foster disintegration of family or community, or function as an instrument of social domination. Second, persons created in the image of God must not become mere accessories of machines. Third, as God's stewards, we must not allow technology to abuse creation. If human work is to be done in cooperation with creation then the instruments of work must cooperate with it too. Finally, we should not allow technological advancements to become objects of false worship or seduce us away from dependence on God (Gen. 11:1-9). We may differ in the weight we ascribe to individual criteria in concrete situations and therefore our assessment of particular technologies may differ. But we believe that these criteria need to be taken into consideration as we reflect theologically on technological progress.

11. We urge individuals, private institutions, and governments everywhere to consider both the local, immediate, and the global, long-term ecological consequences of their actions. We encourage corporate action to make products which are more "environmentally friendly." And we call on governments to create and enforce just frameworks of incentives and penalties which will encourage both individuals and corporations to adopt ecologically sound practices.

12. We need greater international cooperation between individuals, private organizations, and nations to promote environmentally responsible action. Since political action usually serves the self-interest of the powerful, it will be especially important to guarantee that international environmental agreements are particularly concerned to protect the needs of the poor. We call on Christians everywhere to place high priority on restoring and maintaining the integrity of creation.

B. Work and Leisure

Work and Human Nature

13. Work involves all those activities done not for their own sake but to satisfy human needs. Work belongs to the very purpose for which God originally made human beings. In Genesis 1:26-28, we read that God created human beings in his image "in order to have dominion over . . . all the earth." Similarly, Genesis 2:15 tells us that God created Adam and placed him in the Garden of Eden to work in it, to "till it and keep it." As human beings fulfill this mandate, they glorify God. Though fallen, as human beings "go forth to their work" (Ps. 104:23) they fulfill an original purpose of the Creator for human existence.

14. Because work is central to the Creator's intention for humanity, work has intrinsic value. Thus work is not solely a means to an end. It is not simply a chore to be endured for the sake of satisfying human desires or needs, especially the consumption of goods. At the same time, we have to guard against overvaluation of work. The essence of human beings consists in that they are made in the image of God. Their ultimate, but not exclusive, source of meaning and identity does not lie in work, but in becoming children of God by one Spirit through faith in Jesus Christ.

15. For Christians, work acquires a new dimension. God calls all Christians to employ through work the various gifts that God has given them. God calls people to enter the kingdom of God and to live a life in accordance with its demands. When people respond to the call of God, God enables them to bear the fruit of the Spirit and endows them individually with multiple gifts of the Spirit. As those who are gifted by the Spirit and whose actions are guided by the demands of love, Christians should do their work in the service of God and humanity.

The Purpose of Work

16. In the Bible and in the first centuries of the Christian tradition, meeting one's needs and the needs of one's community (especially its underprivileged members) was an essential purpose of work (Ps. 128:2; 2 Thess. 3:8; 1 Thess. 4:9-12; Eph. 4:28; Acts 20:33-35). The first thing at issue in all fields of human work is the need of human beings to earn their daily bread and a little more.

17. The deepest meaning of human work is that the almighty God established human work as a means to accomplish God's work in the world. Human beings remain dependent on God, for "unless the Lord builds the house, those who build it labor in vain" (Ps. 127:1a). As Genesis 2:5 suggests, God and human beings are colaborers in the task of preserving creation.

18. Human work has consequences that go beyond the preservation of creation to the anticipation of the eschatological transformation of the world. They are, of course, not ushering in the kingdom of God, building the "new heavens and a new earth." Only God can do that. Yet their work makes a small and imperfect contribution to it—for example, by shaping the personalities of the citizens of the eternal kingdom which will come through God's action alone.

19. However, work is not only a means through which the glory of human beings as God's stewards shines forth. It is also a place where the misery of human beings as impeders of God's purposes becomes visible. Like the test of fire, God's judgment will bring to light the work which has ultimate significance because it was done in cooperation with God. But it will also manifest the ultimate insignificance of work done in cooperation with those evil powers which scheme to ruin God's good creation (1 Cor. 3:12-15).

Alienation in Work

20. Sin makes work an ambiguous reality. It is both a noble

expression of human creation in the image of God and, because of the curse, a painful testimony to human estrangement from God. Whether human beings are tilling the soil in agrarian societies or operating high-tech machinery in information societies, they work under the shadow of death and experience struggle and frustration in work (Gen. 3:17-19).

21. Human beings are created by God as persons endowed with gifts which God calls them to exercise freely. As a fundamental dimension of human existence, work is a personal activity. People should never be treated in their work as mere means. We must resist the tendency to treat workers merely as costs or labor inputs, a tendency evident in both rural and urban societies, but especially where industrial and postindustrial methods of production are applied. We encourage efforts to establish managerial and technological conditions that enable workers to participate meaningfully in significant decision-making processes, and to create opportunities for individual development by designing positions that challenge them to develop their potential and by instituting educational programs.

22. God gives talents to individuals for the benefit of the whole community. Human work should be a contribution to the common good (Eph. 4:28). The modern drift from concern for community to preoccupation with self, supported by powerful structural and cultural forces, shapes the way we work. Individual self-interest can legitimately be pursued, but only in a context marked by the pursuit of the good of others. These two pursuits are complementary. In order to make the pursuit of the common good possible, Christians need to seek to change both the attitudes of workers and the structures in which they work.

23. Discrimination in work continues to oppress people, especially women and marginalized groups. Because of race and gen-

der, people are often pushed into a narrow range of occupations which are often underpaid, offer little status or security, and provide few promotional opportunities and fringe benefits. Women and men and people of all races are equal before God and should, therefore, be recognized and treated with equal justice and dignity in social and economic life.

24. For most people work is an arduous good. Many workers suffer greatly under the burden of work. In some situations people work long hours for low pay, working conditions are appalling, contracts are nonexistent, sexual harassment occurs, trade union representation is not allowed, health and safety regulations are flouted. These things occur throughout the world whatever the economic system. The word "exploitation" has a strong and immediate meaning in such situations. The God of the Bible condemns exploitation and oppression. God's liberation of the Israelites from their oppression served as a paradigm of how God's people should behave toward workers in their midst (Lev. 25:39-55).

25. Since work is central to God's purpose for humanity, people everywhere have both the obligation and the right to work. Given the broad definition of work suggested above (cf. Para. 13), the right to work here should be understood as part of the freedom of the individual to contribute to the satisfaction of the needs of the community. It is a freedom right, since work in its widest sense is a form of self-expression. The right involved is the right of the worker to work unhindered. The obligation is on every human being to contribute to the community. It is in this sense that Paul says, "If a man will not work, let him not eat."

26. The right to earn a living would be a positive or sustenance right. Such a right implies the obligation of the community to provide employment opportunities. Employment cannot be guar-

anteed where rights conflict and resources may be inadequate. However, the fact that such a right cannot be enforced does not detract in any way from the obligation to seek the highest level of employment which is consistent with justice and the availability of resources.

Rest and Leisure

27. As the Sabbath commandment indicates, the biblical concept of rest should not be confused with the modern concept of leisure. Leisure consists of activities that are ends in themselves and therefore intrinsically enjoyable. In many parts of the world for many people, life is "all work and no play." While masses of people are unemployed and thus have only "leisure," millions of people—including children—are often overworked simply to meet their basic survival needs. Meanwhile, especially in economically developed nations, many overwork to satisfy their desire for status.

28. The first pages of the Bible tell us that God rested after creating the universe (Gen. 2:2-3). The sequence of work and rest that we see in God's activity is a pattern for human beings. In that the Sabbath commandment interrupted work with regular periods of rest, it liberates human beings from enslavement to work. The Sabbath erects a fence around human productive activity and serves to protect both human and nonhuman creation. Human beings have, therefore, both a right and an obligation to rest.

29. Corresponding to the four basic relations in which all people stand (in relationship to nonhuman creation, to themselves, to other human beings, and to God), there are four activities which we should cultivate in leisure time. Rest consists in the enjoyment of nature as God's creation, in the free exercise and development of abilities which God has given to each person, in the cultivation of fellowship with one another, and above all, in delight in com-

munion with God.

30. Worship is central to the biblical concept of rest. In order to be truly who they are, human beings need periodic moments of time in which God's commands concerning their work will recede from the forefront of their consciousness as they adore the God of loving holiness and thank the God of holy love.

31. Those who cannot meet their basic needs without having to forgo leisure can be encouraged by the reality of their right to rest. The right to rest implies the corresponding right to sustenance for all those who are willing to work "six days a week" (Ex. 20:9). Modern workaholics whose infatuation with status relegates leisure to insignificance must be challenged by the liberating obligation to rest. What does it profit them to "gain the whole world" if they "forfeit their life" (Mark 8:36)?

C. Poverty and Justice

God and the Poor

32. Poverty was not part of God's original creation, nor will poverty be part of God's restored creation when Christ returns. Involuntary poverty in all its forms and manifestations is a result of the fall and its consequences. Today one of every five human beings lives in poverty so extreme that his or her survival is daily in doubt. We believe this is offensive and heartbreaking to God.

33. We understand that the God of the Bible is one who in mercy extends love to all. At the same time, we believe that when the poor are oppressed, God is the "defender of the poor" (Ps. 146:7–9). Again and again in every part of Scripture, the Bible expresses God's concern for justice for the poor. Faithful obedience requires that we share God's concern and act on it. "He who oppresses a poor man insults his maker, but he who is kind to the needy

honors Him" (Prov. 14:31). Indeed it is only when we right such injustices that God promises to hear our prayers and worship (Isa. 58:1–9).

34. Neglect of the poor often flows from greed. Furthermore, the obsessive or careless pursuit of material goods is one of the most destructive idolatries in human history (Eph. 5:5). It distracts individuals from their duties before God and corrupts personal and social relationships.

Causes of Poverty

35. The causes of poverty are many and complex. They include the evil that people do to each other, to themselves, and to their environment. The causes of poverty also include the cultural attitudes and actions taken by social, economic, political and religious institutions that either devalue or waste resources, that erect barriers to economic production, or that fail to reward work fairly. Furthermore, the forces that cause and perpetuate poverty operate at global, national, local and personal levels. It is also true that a person may be poor because of sickness, mental or physical handicap, childhood, or old age. Poverty is also caused by natural disasters such as earthquakes, hurricanes, floods, and famines.

36. We recognize that poverty results from and is sustained by both constraints on the production of wealth and the inequitable distribution of wealth and income. We acknowledge the tendency we have had to reduce the causes of poverty to one at the expense of the other. We affirm the need to analyze and explain the conditions that promote the creation of wealth, as well as those that determine the distribution of wealth.

37. We believe it is the responsibility of every society to provide people with the means to live at a level consistent with their standing as persons created in the image of God.

Justice and Poverty

38. Biblical justice means impartially rendering to everyone their due in conformity with the standards of God's moral law. Paul uses justice (or righteousness) in its most comprehensive sense as a metaphor to describe God's creative and powerful redemptive love. Christ, solely in grace, brought us into God's commonwealth, who were strangers to it and because of sin cut off from it (Rom. 1:17-18; 3:21-26; Eph. 2:4-22). In biblical passages which deal with the distribution of the benefits of social life in the context of social conflict and social wrong, justice is related particularly to what is due to groups such as the poor, widows, orphans, resident aliens, wage earners and slaves. The common link among these groups is powerlessness by virtue of economic and social needs. The justice called forth is to restore these groups to the provision God intends for them. God's law expresses this justice and indicates its demands. Further, God's intention is for people to live, not in isolation, but in society. The poor are described as those who are weak with respect to the rest of the community; the responsibility of the community is stated as "to make them strong" so that they can continue to take their place in the community (Lev. 25:35-36). One of the dilemmas of the poor is their loss of community (Job 22:5; Ps. 107:4-9, 33-36). Indeed, their various needs are those that tend to prevent people from being secure and contributing members of society. One essential characteristic of biblical justice is the meeting of basic needs that have been denied in contradiction to the standards of Scripture; but further, the Bible gives indication of how to identify which needs are basic. They are those essential, not just for life, but for life in society.

39. Justice requires special attention to the weak members of the community because of their greater vulnerability. In this sense,

justice is partial. Nevertheless, the civil arrangements in rendering justice are not to go beyond what is due to the poor or to the rich (Deut. 1:17; Lev. 19:15). In this sense justice is ultimately impartial. Justice is so fundamental that it characterizes the personal virtues and personal relationships of individuals as they faithfully follow God's standards. Those who violate God's standards, however, receive God's retributive justice, which often removes the offender from society or from the divine community.

40. Justice requires conditions such that each person is able to participate in society in a way compatible with human dignity. Absolute poverty, where people lack even minimal food and housing, basic education, health care, and employment, denies people the basic economic resources necessary for just participation in the community. Corrective action with and on behalf of the poor is a necessary act of justice. This entails responsibilities for individuals, families, churches, and governments.

41. Justice may also require sociopolitical actions that enable the poor to help themselves and be the subjects of their own development and the development of their communities. We believe that we and the institutions in which we participate are responsible to create an environment of law, economic activity, and spiritual nurture which creates these conditions.

Some Urgent Contemporary Issues

42. Inequitable international economic relations aggravate poverty in poor countries. Many of these countries suffer under a burden of debt service which could only be repaid at an unacceptable price to the poor, unless there is a radical restructuring of both national economic policies and international economic relations. The combination of increasing interest rates and falling commodity prices in the early 1980s has increased this debt serv-

ice burden. Both lenders and borrowers shared in creating this debt. The result has been increasing impoverishment of the people. Both lenders and borrowers must share responsibility for finding solutions. We urgently encourage governments and international financial institutions to redouble their efforts to find ways to reduce the international indebtedness of the Third World, and to ensure the flow of both private and public productive capital where appropriate.

43. Government barriers to the flow of goods and services often work to the disadvantage of the poor. We particularly abhor the protectionist policies of the wealthy nations which are detrimental to developing countries. Greater freedom of trade between nations is an important part of reducing poverty worldwide.

44. Justice requires that the value of money be reliably known and stable; thus inflation represents poor stewardship and defrauds the nations' citizens. It wastes resources and is particularly harmful to the poor and the powerless. The wealthier members of society find it much easier to protect themselves against inflation than do the poor. Rapid changes in prices drastically affect the ability of the poor to purchase basic goods.

45. Annual global military expenditures equal the annual income of the poorest one-half of the world's people. These vast, excessive military expenditures detract from the task of meeting basic human needs, such as food, health care, and education. We are encouraged by the possibilities represented by the changes in the USSR and Eastern Europe, and improving relations between East and West. We urge that a major part of the resulting "peace dividend" be used to provide sustainable solutions to the problems of the world's poor.

46. Drug use and trafficking destroy both rich and poor nations. Drug consumption reflects spiritual poverty among the people and

societies in which drug use is apparent. Drug trafficking undermines the national economies of those who produce drugs. The economic, social, and spiritual costs of drug use are unacceptable. The two key agents involved in this problem must change: the rich markets which consume drugs and the poorer countries which produce them. Therefore both must urgently work to find solutions. The rich markets which consume drugs must end their demand. And the poorer countries which produce them must switch to other products.

47. We deplore economic systems based on policies, laws and regulations whose effect is to favor privileged minorities and to exclude the poor from fully legitimate activities. Such systems are not only inefficient but immoral as well in that participating in and benefiting from the formal economy depends on conferred privilege of those who have access and influence to public and private institutions rather than on inventiveness and hard work. Actions need to be taken by public and private institutions to reduce and simplify the requirements and costs of participating in the national economy.

48. There is abundant evidence that investment in small-scale enterprises run by and for the poor can have a positive impact upon income and job creation for the poor. Contrary to the myths upheld by traditional financial institutions, the poor are often good entrepreneurs and excellent credit risks. We deplore the lack of credit available to the poor in the informal sector. We strongly encourage governments, financial institutions, and nongovernmental organizations to redouble their efforts to significantly increase credit to the poor. We feel so strongly about this that a separate statement dedicated to credit-based income generation programs has been issued by the conference.

D. Freedom, Government and Economics

The Language of Human Rights

49. With the United Nations Declaration of Human Rights, the language of human rights has become pervasive throughout the world. It expresses the urgent plight of suffering people whose humanity is daily being denied them by their oppressors. In some cases rights language has been misused by those who claim that anything they want is theirs "by right." This breadth of application has led some to reject rights as a concept, stating that if everything becomes a right then nothing will be a right, since all rights imply corresponding responsibilities. Therefore it is important to have clear criteria for what defines rights.

Christian Distinctives

50. All human interaction is judged by God and is accountable to God. In seeking human rights we search for an authority or norm which transcends our situation. God is that authority; God's character constitutes that norm. Since human rights are a priori rights, they are not conferred by the society or the state. Rather, human rights are rooted in the fact that every human being is made in the image of God. The deepest ground of human dignity is that while we were yet sinners, Christ died for us (Rom. 5:8).

51. In affirmation of the dignity of God's creatures, God's justice for them requires life, freedom, and sustenance. The divine requirements of justice establish corresponding rights for human beings to whom justice is due. The right to life is the most basic human right. God created human beings as free moral agents. As such, they have the right to freedom—e.g., freedom of religion, speech, and assembly. Their freedom, however, is properly used only in dependence on God. It is a requirement of justice that

human beings, including refugees and stateless persons, are able to live in society with dignity. Human beings therefore have a claim on other human beings for social arrangements that ensure that they have access to the sustenance that makes life in society possible.

52. The fact that in becoming Christians we may choose to forgo our rights out of love for others and in trust of God's providential care does not mean that such rights cease to exist. Christians may endure the violation of their rights with great courage but work vigorously for the identical rights of others in similar circumstances. However, it may not be appropriate to do so in some circumstances. Indeed this disparity between Christian contentment and campaigning on behalf of others in adverse situations is a witness to the work and love of God.

53. All of us share the same aspirations as human beings to have our rights protected—whether the right to life, freedom, or sustenance. Yet the fact of sin and the conflict of competing human rights means that our aspirations are never completely fulfilled in this life. Through Christ, sin and evil have been conquered. They will remain a destructive force until the consummation of all things. But that in no way reduces our horror at the widespread violation of human rights today.

Democracy

54. As a model, modern political democracy is characterized by limited government of a temporary character, by the division of power within the government, the distinction between state and society, pluralism, the rule of law, institutionalization of freedom rights (including free and regular elections), and a significant amount of nongovernmental control of property. We recognize that no political system is directly prescribed by Scripture, but we

believe that biblical values and historical experience call Christians to work for the adequate participation of all people in the decision-making processes on questions that affect their lives.

55. We also recognize that simply to vote periodically is not a sufficient expression of democracy. For a society to be truly democratic, economic power must be shared widely, and class and status distinctions must not be barriers preventing access to economic and social institutions. Democracies are also open to abuse through the very channels which make them democratic. Small, economically powerful groups sometimes dominate the political process. Democratic majorities can be swayed by materialistic, racist, or nationalistic sentiments to engage in unjust policies. The fact that all human institutions are fallen means that the people must be constantly alert to and critical of all that is wrong.

56. We recognize that no particular economic system is directly prescribed by Scripture. Recent history suggests that a dispersion of ownership of the means of production is a significant component of democracy. Monopolistic ownership by the state, large economic institutions, or oligarchies is dangerous. Widespread ownership, either in a market economy or in a mixed system, tends to decentralize power and prevent totalitarianism.

The Concentration of Economic Power

57. Economic power can be concentrated in the hands of a few people in a market economy. When that occurs political decisions tend to be made for economic reasons, and the average member of the society is politically and economically marginalized. Control over economic life may thus be far removed from a large part of the population. Transnational corporations can also wield enormous influence on some economies. Despite these problems, economic power is diffused within market-oriented economies to a

greater extent than in other systems.

58. In centrally planned economies, economic decisions are made for political reasons, people's economic choices are curtailed, and the economy falters. Heavy state involvement and regulation within market economies can also result in concentrations of power that effectively marginalize poorer members of the society. Corruption almost inevitably follows from concentrated economic power. Widespread corruption so undermines society that there is a virtual breakdown of legitimate order.

Capitalism and Culture

59. As noncapitalist countries increasingly turn away from central planning and toward the market, the question of capitalism's effect on culture assumes more and more importance. The market system can be an effective means of economic growth, but can, in the process, cause people to think that ultimate meaning is found in the accumulation of more goods. The overwhelming consumerism of Western societies is testimony to the fact that the material success of capitalism encourages forces and attitudes that are decidedly non-Christian. One such attitude is the treatment of workers as simply costs or productive inputs, without recognition of their humanity. There is also the danger that the model of the market, which may work well in economic transactions, will be assumed to be relevant to other areas of life, and people may consequently believe that what the market encourages is therefore best or most true.

The Role of Government

60. Government is designed to serve the purposes of God to foster community, particularly in response to our rebellious nature (Rom. 13:1, 4; Ps. 72:1). As an institution administered by human

beings, government can exacerbate problems of power, greed, and envy. However, it can, where properly constructed and constrained, serve to limit some of these sinful tendencies. Therefore, it is the responsibility of Christians to work for governmental structures that serve justice. Such structures must respect the principle that significant decisions about local human communities are usually best made at a level of government most directly responsible to the people affected.

61. At a minimum, government must establish a rule of law that protects life, secures freedom, and provides basic security. Special care must be taken to make sure the protection of fundamental rights is extended to all members of society, especially the poor and oppressed (Prov. 31:8-9; Dan. 4:27). Too often government institutions are captured by the economically or socially powerful. Thus, equality before the law fails to exist for those without power. Government must also have regard for economic efficiency and appropriately limit its own scope and action.

62. The provision of sustenance rights is also an appropriate function of government. Such rights must be carefully defined so that government's involvement will not encourage irresponsible behavior and the breakdown of families and communities. In a healthy society, this fulfillment of rights will be provided through a diversity of institutions so that the government's role will be that of last resort.

Mediating Structures

63. One of the phenomena associated with the modern world is the increasing divide between private and public sectors. The need for a bridge between these two sectors has led to an emphasis on mediating institutions. The neighborhood, the family, the church and other voluntary associations are all such institutions.

As the early church did in its context, these institutions provide citizens with many opportunities for loyalty in addition to the state and the family. Their role in meeting the needs of members of the community decreases the need for centralized government. They also provide a channel for individuals to influence government, business, and other large institutions. Therefore Christians should encourage governments everywhere to foster vigorous voluntary associations.

64. The future of poverty alleviation is likely to involve expanded microeconomic income generation programs and entrepreneurial development of the so-called informal sector as it becomes part of the transformed formal economy. In this context, there will most likely be an even greater role for nongovernmental organizations. In particular, church bodies will be able to make a significant and creative contribution in partnership with the poor, acting as mediating institutions by virtue of the churches' longstanding grassroots involvement in local communities.

Conclusion

65. As we conclude, we thank God for the opportunity God has given us to participate in this conference. Through our time together we have been challenged to express our faith in the area of economic life in practical ways. We acknowledge that all too often we have allowed society to shape our views and actions and have failed to apply scriptural teaching in this crucial area of our lives, and we repent.

We now encourage one another to uphold Christian economic values in the face of unjust and subhuman circumstances. We realize, however, that ethical demands are often ineffective because they are reinforced only by individual conscience and that the proclamation of Christian values needs to be accompanied by action to encourage institutional and structural changes which would foster these values in our communities. We will therefore endeavor to seek every opportunity to work for the implementation of the principles outlined in this Declaration, in faithfulness to God's calling.

We urge all people, and especially Christians, to adopt stewardship and justice as the guiding principles for all aspects of economic life, particularly for the sake of those who are most vulnerable. These principles must be applied in all spheres of life. They have to do with our use of material resources and lifestyle as well as with the way people and nations relate to one another. With girded loins and burning lamps we wait for the return of our Lord Jesus Christ when justice and peace shall embrace.

The Lausanne Covenant

Introduction

We, members of the church of Jesus Christ, from more than 150 nations, participants in the International Congress on World Evangelization at Lausanne, praise God for his great salvation and rejoice in the fellowship he has given us with himself and with each other. We are deeply stirred by what God is doing in our day, moved to penitence by our failures and challenged by the unfinished task of evangelization. We believe the gospel is God's good news for the whole world, and we are determined by his grace to obey Christ's commission to proclaim it to all mankind and to make disciples of every nation. We desire, therefore, to affirm our faith and our resolve, and to make public our covenant.

1. The Purpose of God

We affirm our belief in the one eternal God, Creator and Lord of the world, Father, Son and Holy Spirit, who governs all things according to the purpose of his will. He has been calling out from the world a people for himself, and sending his people back into the world to be his servants and his witnesses, for the extension of his kingdom, the building up of Christ's body, and the glory of his name. We confess with shame that we have often denied our calling and failed in our mission, by becoming conformed to the world or by withdrawing from it. Yet we rejoice that even when borne by earthen vessels the gospel is still a precious treasure. To the task of making that treasure known in the power of the Holy Spirit we desire to dedicate ourselves anew. (Isa. 40:28; Matt. 28:19; Eph. 1:11; Acts 15:14; John 17:6, 18; Eph. 4:12; 1 Cor. 5:10; Rom. 12:2; 2 Cor. 4:7)

2. The Authority and Power of the Bible

We affirm the divine inspiration, truthfulness and authority of both Old and New Testament Scriptures in their entirety as the only written word of God, without error in all that it affirms, and the only infallible rule of faith and practice. We also affirm the power of God's Word to accomplish his purpose of salvation. The message of the Bible is addressed to all mankind. For God's revelation in Christ and in Scripture is unchangeable. Through it the Holy Spirit still speaks today. He illumines the minds of God's people in every culture to perceive its truth freshly through their own eyes and thus discloses to the whole church ever more of the many-colored wisdom of God. (2 Tim. 3:16; 2 Pet. 1:21; John 10:35; Isa. 55:11; 1 Cor. 1:21; Rom. 1:16; Matt. 5:17-18; Jude 3; Eph. 1:17-18; 3:10, 18)

3. The Uniqueness and Universality of Christ

We affirm that there is only one Savior and only one gospel, although there is a wide diversity of evangelistic approaches. We recognize that all men have some knowledge of God through his general revelation in nature. But we deny that this can save, for men suppress the truth by their unrighteousness. We also reject as derogatory to Christ and the gospel every kind of syncretism and dialogue which implies that Christ speaks equally through all religions and ideologies. Jesus Christ, being himself the only God-man, who gave himself as the only ransom for sinners, is the only mediator between God and man. There is no other name by which we must be saved. All men are perishing because of sin, but God loves all men, not wishing that any should perish but that all should repent. Yet those who reject Christ repudiate the joy of salvation and condemn themselves to eternal separation from God. To proclaim Jesus as "the Savior of the world" is not to affirm that all men are either automatically or ultimately saved, still less to affirm that all religions offer salvation in Christ. Rather it is to proclaim God's love for a world of sinners and to invite all men to respond to him as Savior and Lord in the wholehearted personal commitment of repentance and faith. Jesus Christ has been exalted above every other name; we long for the day when every knee shall bow to him and every tongue shall confess him Lord. (Gal. 1:6-9; Rom. 1:18-32; 1 Tim. 2:5-6; Acts 4:12; John 3:16-19; 2 Pet. 3:9; 2 Thess. 1:7-9; John 4:42; Matt. 11:28; Eph. 1:20-21; Phil. 2:9-11)

4. The Nature of Evangelism

To evangelize is to spread the good news that Jesus Christ died for our sins and was raised from the dead according to the Scriptures, and that as the reigning Lord he now offers the forgiveness of sins and the liberating gift of the Spirit to all who repent and believe. Our Christian presence in the world is indispensable to evangelism, and so is that kind of dialogue whose purpose is to listen sensitively in order to understand. But evangelism itself is the proclamation of the historical, biblical Christ as Savior and Lord, with a view to persuading people to come to him personally and so be reconciled to God. In issuing the gospel invitation we have no liberty to conceal the cost of discipleship. Jesus still calls all who would follow him to deny themselves, take up their cross, and identify themselves with his new community. The results of evangelism include obedience to Christ, incorporation into his church and responsible service in the world.

5. Christian Social Responsibility

We affirm that God is both the Creator and the Judge of all men. We therefore should share his concern for justice and reconciliation throughout human society and for the liberation of men from every kind of oppression. Because mankind is made in the image of God, every person, regardless of race, religion, color, culture, class, sex or age, has an intrinsic dignity because of which he should be respected and served, not exploited. Here too we express penitence both for our neglect and for having sometimes regarded evangelism and social concern as mutually exclusive. Although reconciliation with man is not reconciliation with God, nor is social action evangelism, nor is political liberation salvation, nevertheless we affirm that evangelism and sociopolitical involvement are both part of our Christian duty. For both are necessary expressions of our doctrines of God and man, our love for our neighbor and our obedience to Jesus Christ. The message of salvation implies also a message of judgment upon every form of alienation, oppression and discrimination, and we should not be afraid to denounce evil and injustice wherever they exist. When people receive Christ they are born again into his kingdom and must seek not only to exhibit but also to spread its righteousness in the midst of an unrighteous world. The salvation we claim should be transforming us in the totality of our personal and social responsibilities. Faith without works is dead. (Acts 17:26, 31; Gen. 18:25; Isa. 1:17; Ps. 45:7; Gen. 1:26–27; James 3:9; Lev. 19:18; Luke 6:27, 35; James 2:14-26; John 3:3, 5; Matt. 5:20; 6:33; 2 Cor. 3:18; James 2:20)

6. The Church and Evangelism

We affirm that Christ sends his redeemed people into the world as the Father sent him, and that this calls for a similar deep and costly penetration of the world. We need to break out of our ecclesiastical ghettos and permeate non-Christian society. In the church's mission of sacrificial service evangelism is primary. World evangelization requires the whole church to take the whole gospel to the whole world. The church is at the very center of God's cosmic purpose and is his appointed means of spreading the gospel. But a church which preaches the cross must itself be marked by the cross. It becomes a stumbling block to evangelism when it betrays the gospel or lacks a living faith in God, a genuine love for people, or scrupulous honesty in all things including promotion and finance. The church is the community of God's people rather than an institution and must not be identified with any particular culture, social or political system, or human ideology. (John 17:18; 20:21; Matt. 28:19-20; Acts 1:8; 20:27; Eph. 1:9-10; 3:9-11; Gal. 6:14, 17; 2 Cor. 6:3-4; 2 Tim. 2:19-21; Phil. 1:27)

7. Cooperation in Evangelism

We affirm that the church's visible unity in truth is God's purpose. Evangelism also summons us to unity, because our oneness strengthens our witness, just as our disunity undermines our gospel of reconciliation. We recognize, however, that organizational unity may take many forms and does not necessarily forward evangelism. Yet we who share the same biblical faith should be closely united in fellowship, work and witness. We confess that our testimony has sometimes been marred by sinful individualism and needless duplication. We pledge ourselves to seek a deeper unity in truth, worship, holiness and mission. We urge the development of regional and functional cooperation for the furtherance of the church's mission, for strategic planning, for mutual encouragement, and for the sharing of resources and experience. (John 17:21, 23; Eph. 4:3-4; John 13:35; Phil. 1:27; John 17:11-23)

8. Churches in Evangelistic Partnership

We rejoice that a new missionary era has dawned. The dominant role of Western mission is fast disappearing. God is raising up from the younger churches a great new resource for world evangelization, and is thus demonstrating that the responsibility to evangelize belongs to the whole body of Christ. All churches should therefore be asking God and themselves what they should be doing both to reach their own area and to send missionaries to other parts of the world. A reevaluation of our missionary responsibility and role should be continuous. Thus a growing partnership of churches will develop and the universal character of Christ's church will be more clearly exhibited. We also thank God for agencies which labor in Bible translation, theological education, the mass media, Christian literature, evangelism, missions, church renewal and other specialist fields. They too should engage in constant self-examination to evaluate their effectiveness as part of the church's mission. (Rom 1:8; Phil. 1:5; 4:15; Acts 13:1-3; 1 Thess. 1:6-8)

9. The Urgency of the Evangelistic Task

More than 2,700 million people, which is more than two-thirds of mankind, have yet to be evangelized. We are ashamed that so many have been neglected; it is a standing rebuke to us and to the whole church. There is now, however, in many parts of the world an unprecedented receptivity to the Lord Jesus Christ. We are convinced that this is the time for churches and parachurch agencies to pray earnestly for the salvation of the unreached and to launch new efforts to achieve world evangelization. A reduction of foreign missionaries and money in an evangelized country may sometimes be necessary to facilitate the national church's growth in self-reliance and to release resources for unevangelized areas. Missionaries should flow ever more freely from and to all six continents in a spirit of humble service. The goal should be, by all available means and at the earliest possible time, that every person will have the opportunity to hear, understand, and receive the Good News. We cannot hope to attain this goal without sacrifice. All of us are shocked by the poverty of millions and disturbed by the injustices which cause it. Those of us who live in affluent circumstances accept our duty to develop a simple lifestyle in order to contribute more generously to both relief and evangelism.

10. Evangelism and Culture

The development of strategies for world evangelization calls for imaginative pioneering methods. Under God, the result will be the rise of churches deeply rooted in Christ and closely related to their culture. Culture must always be tested and judged by Scripture. Because man is God's creature, some of his culture is rich in beauty and goodness. Because he is fallen, all of it is tainted with sin and some of it is demonic. The gospel does not presuppose the superiority of any culture to another, but evaluates all cultures according to its own criteria of truth and righteousness, and insists on moral absolutes in every culture. Missions have all too frequently exported with the gospel an alien culture, and churches have sometimes been in bondage to culture rather than to the Scripture. Christ's evangelists must humbly seek to empty themselves of all but their personal authenticity in order to become the servants of others, and churches must seek to transform and enrich culture, all for the glory of God. (Mark 7:8-9, 13; Gen. 4:21-22; 1 Cor. 9:19-23; Phil. 2:5-7; 2 Cor. 4:5)

11. Education and Leadership

We confess that we have sometimes pursued church growth at the expense of church depth, and divorced evangelism from Christian nurture. We also acknowledge that some of our missions have been too slow to equip and encourage national leaders to assume their rightful responsibilities. Yet we are committed to indigenous principles and long that every church will have national leaders who manifest a Christian style of leadership in terms not of domination but of service. We recognize that there is a great need to improve theological education, especially for church leaders. In every nation and culture there should be an effective training program for pastors and laymen in doctrine, discipleship, evangelism, nurture and service. Such training programs should not rely on any stereotyped methodology but should be developed by creative local initiatives according to biblical standards. (Col. 1:27-28; Acts 14:23; Tit. 1:5, 9; Mark 10:42-45; Eph. 4:11-12)

12. Spiritual Conflict

We believe that we are engaged in constant spiritual warfare with the principalities and powers of evil, who are seeking to overthrow the church and frustrate its task of world evangelization. We know our need to equip ourselves with God's armor and to fight this battle with the spiritual weapons of truth and prayer. For we detect the activity of our enemy, not only in false ideologies outside the church, but also inside it in false gospels which twist Scripture and put man in the place of God. We need both watchfulness and discernment to safeguard the biblical gospel. We acknowledge that we ourselves are not immune to worldliness of thought and action, that is, to a surrender to secularism. For example, although careful studies of church growth, both numerical and spiritual, are right and valuable, we have sometimes neglected them. At other times, desirous to ensure a response to the gospel, we have compromised our message, manipulated our hearers through pressure techniques, and become unduly preoccupied with statistics or even dishonest in our use of them. All this is worldly. The church must be in the world; the world must not be in the church. (Eph. 6:12; 2 Cor. 4:3-4; Eph. 6:11, 13-18; 2 Cor. 10:3-5; 1 John 2:18-26; 4:1-3; Gal. 1:6-9; 2 Cor. 2:17; 4:2; John 17:15)

13. Freedom and Persecution

It is the God-appointed duty of every government to secure conditions of peace, justice and liberty in which the church may obey God, serve the Lord Christ, and preach the gospel without interference. We therefore pray for the leaders of the nations and call upon them to guarantee freedom of thought and conscience, and freedom to practice and propagate religion in accordance with the will of God and as set for the Universal Declaration of Human Rights. We also express our deep concern for all who have been unjustly imprisoned, and especially for our brethren who are suffering for their testimony to the Lord Jesus. We promise to pray and work for their freedom. At the same time we refuse to be intimidated by their fate. God helping us, we too will seek to stand against injustice and to remain faithful to the gospel, whatever the cost. We do not forget the warnings of Jesus that persecution is inevitable. (1 Tim. 1:1–4; Acts 4:19; 5:29; Col. 3:24; Heb. 13:1–3; Luke 4:18; Gal. 5:11; 6:12; Matt. 5:10–12; John 15:18–21)

14. The Power of the Holy Spirit

We believe in the power of the Holy Spirit. The Father sent his Spirit to bear witness to his Son; without his witness ours is futile. Conviction of sin, faith in Christ, new birth and Christian growth are all his work. Further, the Holy Spirit is a missionary spirit; thus evangelism should arise spontaneously from a Spirit-filled church. A church that is not a missionary church is contradicting itself and quenching the Spirit. Worldwide evangelization will become a realistic possibility only when the Spirit renews the church in truth and wisdom, faith, holiness, love and power. We therefore call upon all Christians to pray for such a visitation of the sovereign Spirit of God that all his fruit may appear in all his people and that all his gifts may enrich the body of Christ. Only then will the whole church become a fit instrument in his hands, that the whole earth may hear his voice. (1 Cor. 2:4; John 15:26–27; 16:8–11; 1 Cor. 12:3; John 3:6–8; 2 Cor. 3:18; John 7:37–39; 1 Thess. 5:19; Acts 1:8; Ps. 85:4–7; 67:1–3; Gal. 5:22–23; 1 Cor. 12:4–31; Rom. 12:3–8)

15. The Return of Christ

We believe that Jesus Christ will return personally and visibly, in power and glory, to consummate his salvation and his judgment. This promise of his coming is a further spur to our evangelism, for we remember his words that the gospel must first be preached to all nations. We believe that the interim period between Christ's ascension and return is to be filled with the mission of the people of God, who have no liberty to stop before the End. We also remember his warning that false Christs and false prophets will arise as precursors of the final Antichrist. We therefore reject as a proud, self-confident dream the notion that man can ever build a utopia on earth. Our Christian confidence is that God will perfect his kingdom, and we look forward with eager anticipation to that day, and to the new heaven and earth in which righteousness will dwell and God will reign forever. Meanwhile, we rededicate ourselves to the service of Christ and of men in joyful submission to his authority over the whole of our lives. (Mark 14:62; Heb. 9:28; Mark 13:10; Acts 1:8-11; Matt. 28:20; Mark 13:21-23; John 2:18; 4:1-3; Luke 12:32; Rev. 21:1-5; 2 Pet. 3:13; Matt. 28:18)

Conclusion

Therefore, in the light of this our faith and our resolve, we enter into a solemn covenant with God and with each other, to pray, to plan and to work together for the evangelization of the whole world. We call upon others to join us. May God help us by his grace and for his glory to be faithful to this our covenant! Amen, Alleluia!

Notes

Introduction
[1]Howard A. Snyder, *The Problem of Wineskins: Church Structure in a Technological Age* (Downers Grove, Ill.: InterVarsity Press, 1975).

Chapter One: The Shrinking Globe
[1]A. T. Pierson, *The Divine Enterprise of Missions* (London: Hodder and Stoughton, 1898).

[2]See Harvard economist Robert Reich's article, "Why the Rich Are Getting Richer and the Poor Poorer," *The New Republic*, 1 May 1989, p. 5.

[3]James Risen, *Los Angeles Times*, 12 February 1989.

[4]Jeffrey Gasten, *Current History*, January 1989, p. 15.

[5]Following the events in Tiananmen Square, a replica of China's Lady of Liberty was illegally erected on a bridge in Los Angeles and left there for several days while the city council figured out how to move it without arousing international ire. Full-page ads were taken out in the *New York Times* by the Chinese Democratic Movement, the American Buddhist Confederation and the Central American Days of Decision group to trumpet their respective liberation causes to the American people.

[6]Amy Duncan, "In Music: An International Flavor," *Christian Science Monitor*, 2 January 1990, p. 11.

[7]*Detroit Free Press*, 3 December 1989, p. 4F.

[8]Pierson, *The Crisis of Mission* (New York: Baker and Taylor, 1886).

Chapter Two: The Islamic Revolution
[1]David Lamb, *The Arabs* (New York: Vintage, 1988), pp. 10-11.

[2]"A Frenzied Farewell," *Time*, 19 June 1989, p. 38.

³Atef A. Gawad, "Moscow's Arms-for-Ore Diplomacy," *Foreign Policy* (Summer 1986), p. 147.

⁴Jean-Pierre Langellier, "The March of Islamism," *Le Monde;* reprinted in *World Press Review* (July 1989), p. 30.

⁵Gawad, "Moscow," p. 159.

⁶Sheila Tefft, "Religious Militancy Surges in India," *Christian Science Monitor,* 9 November 1989, p. 4.

⁷Judson Taylor, "Soviet Muslims: Ecological Crisis, *Glasnost,* and the Gospel," *World Christian* 9 (May 1990).

⁸Gawad, "Moscow," p. 164.

⁹Howard LaFranchi, "School Girls in Veils Spark Debate," *The Christian Science Monitor,* 30 October 1989, p. 6.

¹⁰"Americans Facing Toward Mecca," *Time,* 23 May 1988, p. 49.

¹¹Personal interview, 7 April 1990.

Chapter Three: Reaching the World's Poor

¹Of the twenty nations with the highest infant-mortality rate, sixteen are African and four are Asian. Of the twenty nations with the lowest infant-mortality rate, eighteen are Western, two Asian.

²*State of the World's Children* (New York: UNICEF, 1990), p. 37.

³Of the twenty nations with the highest maternal-mortality rate, fourteen are African, five Asian and one Latin American. Of the twenty-one nations with the lowest maternal mortality rates, one is African, two Asian and eighteen Western.

⁴*State of the World's Children,* p. 29.

⁵*World Declaration on Education for All,* presented at the World Conference on Education for All, Thailand, March 1990.

⁶*A Call to Action from the International Task Force on Literacy,* presented by the International Task Force on Literacy, India, October 1989.

⁷Frank Kaleb Jansen, ed., *Target Earth: The Necessity of Diversity in a Wholistic Perspective on World Mission* (Pasadena, Calif.: Global Mapping International, 1989), p. 49.

⁸Ibid., p. 38.

⁹The story is told more fully by Jared Diamond, "The Golden Age That Never Was," *Discover* (December 1989), p. 77.

Chapter Four: The Earth Groans

¹Jared Diamond, "The Golden Age That Never Was," *Discover* (December 1989), p. 77.

[2]Per Worldwatch Institute.

[3]Diamond, "Golden Age," p. 79.

[4]"Bicycles and Buses," *Advocate* (April 1990), p. 1.

[5]John M. Mellor, "Environmental Problems and Poverty," *Environment* (November 1988), p. 28.

[6]Ibid.

[7]Marlise Simons, "Concern Rising over Harm from Pesticides in Third World," *New York Times,* 30 May 1989, p. 21.

[8]Ibid.

[9]Paul Ruffins, "Toxic Terrorism Invades Third World," *Black Enterprise* (November 1988), p. 31.

[10]See Judith Stone, "Toxic Avengers," *Discover* (August 1989), p. 41.

[11]Robert Alvarez and Arjun Makhijani, *Technology Review* (August/September 1988), p. 42.

[12]J. W. Maurits la Riviére, "Threats to the World's Water," *Scientific American* (September 1989), p. 83.

[13]"Trouble on Tap," *Worldwatch* (September/October 1989), p. 12.

[14]Karin Perkins, "Central America's Forgotten Rain Forests," *Christian Science Monitor,* 20 October 1989, p. 19.

[15]Clayton Jones, "Cambodia Turns Giant Hardwoods to Political Profit," *Christian Science Monitor,* 13 November 1989, p. 4.

[16]Eugene Linden, "The Death of Birth," *Time,* 2 January 1989, p. 32.

[17]Joseph K. Sheldon, "Creation Rediscovered," *World Christian* 9 (April 1990).

[18]Ruth Goring Stewart, *Environmental Stewardship* (Downers Grove, Ill.: InterVarsity Press, 1990).

Chapter Five: Setting the Captives Free

[1]Mark Fineman, "Society Crumbling," *Los Angeles Times,* 27 July 1989, p. 9.

[2]Melinda Lin, "Burma's Money Tree," *Newsweek,* 15 May 1989, p. 42.

[3]Mathews K. George, "Nationalism," *South* (January 1989), p. 38.

[4]Taken from personal correspondence with Janine R. Wedel, an Eastern European anthropologist.

Chapter Six: The Urban Challenge

[1]Kathleen Newland, "City Limits: Emerging Constraints on Urban Growth," *Worldwatch Paper* 38 (April 1980), p. 16.

[2]Viv Grigg, in *Urban Mission* (May 1989), p. 43.

[3]*World Press Review* (October 1989), p. 33.

[4]Ibid., p. 34.

[5]Ibid.

[6]Haron Wachira, "The Ghettos of Nairobi: Places of Struggle, Places of Faith," *World Christian* 9 (January 1990):13.

[7]Larry Wilson, *Childlife* (Summer 1989), p. 6.

[8]Ray Bakke, in *Urban Mission* (May 1989), p. 11.

[9]*Youthworker Journal* (Winter 1989), p. 24.

Chapter Seven: The Gorbachev Revolution

[1]Mikhail Gorbachev, quoted in *Time,* 11 December 1989, p. 37.

[2]Ibid.

[3]*Christian Science Monitor,* 18 May 1989, p. 3.

[4]*Current History* (October 1988), p. 321.

[5]"Myths About Lenin," *Christian Science Monitor,* 27 June 1989.

[6]*Time,* 1 January 1990, p. 54.

[7]*Current History,* p. 323.

[8]*Time,* 19 June 1989, p. 28.

[9]*Christian Science Monitor,* 26 May 1989, p. 12.

[10]*Los Angeles Times,* 7 May 1989, p. 1.

[11]Mikhail Gorbachev, *Perestroika: New Thinking for Our Country and the World* (New York: Harper & Row, 1987), pp. 129-30.

[12]*Los Angeles Times,* 4 December 1989, p. B7.

Chapter Eight: The Fading Glory of the West

[1]Harris Morgenthau, quoted in *Current History* (May 1988), p. 34.

[2]Ibid., p. 56.

[3]Thomas Perry Thornton, in the *Annals of the AAAPSS,* p. 10.

[4]Carlos Fuentes, in *The Nation,* 22 March 1986, p. 337.

[5]*Christian Science Monitor,* 21 November 1989, p. 9.

[6]*Christian Science Monitor,* 24 November 1989, p. 8.

[7]Jon Cowan, staffer to Congressman Mel Livine (D-CA).

[8]*Time,* 9 November 1989, p. 68.

[9]*Time,* 12 June 1989, p. 52.

[10]Statistics compiled from *Time,* 12 June 1989, and *Christian Science Monitor,* 30 November 1989 and 18 December 1989.

Chapter Nine: The Evangelism Crisis

[1]David Barrett, ed., *World Christian Encyclopedia* (New York: Oxford University

Press, 1982), pp. 5-6, 8.
[2]Ibid.
[3]From a paper distributed at the annual meeting of Frontier Missions, 1989.
[4]Ibid.
[5]Statistics from *Mission Handbook,* 14th ed. (Monrovia, Calif.: MARC/World Vision, 1989).
[6]Ibid.